To success,

K.S.

Advance Praise for
Life Beyond Time Management

"This is a superb book — compellingly written and loaded with insights that are both practical and profound. The anecdotes and stories are eye-opening and gripping. The research is up-to-the-minute, and the tips and techniques for putting balance into your life really do work. I find the 'mental helicopter' ride the authors suggest to be more exhilarating and revealing than any of the real helicopter rides I've taken."

— Scott DeGarmo, Editor-in-Chief & Publisher
SUCCESS Magazine

"The next step forward in self leadership. The authors wisely counsel that time — much like a chessboard — cannot be managed. Only priorities — like chess pieces — can be moved, over time. It's about balance and winning, where the game is life!"

— Denis Waitley, Ph.D.
Author of *Empires of the Mind*

"This is an extremely practical book written by two experts who have invested many years studying the behaviors of high achieving men and women. It is full of practical, proven principles that you can use immediately to get far more out of every area of your life."

— Brian Tracy
Author of *Maximum Achievement* and *Psychology of Selling*

"In today's hectic, chaotic world, it's easy to lose your focus and achieve far less success and happiness than you are capable of. *Life Beyond Time Management* presents an abundance of excellent ideas and exercises to keep you on track and ensure that you get the most out of life."
— Michael LeBoeuf
Author of *Working Smart* and *The Perfect Business*

"Successful entrepreneurs know how to make use of their most valuable resources: time, energy, and money. In this book, Kim and Willy Norup show you how to go from making a living to *designing your life*. If you're ready to make this exciting leap, this book can show you how!"
— Terri Lonier
Author of *Working Solo*

"*Life Beyond Time Management* presents an incredibly logical and well-articulated approach to planning one's life. It gives you, the reader, a fool-proof process for success — whatever your endeavor. More importantly, it is a means to happiness. I only wish I could have had the opportunity to read and follow the authors' advice much earlier in life. But it's never too late!"
— Roger A. Jones, Brigadier General
United States Air Force–Retired

"A rewarding and valuable resource for managers and leaders, especially those just starting their careers. I would encourage others to read it and live it."
— William P. Sexton, Chief Executive Officer
Mayo Healthcare System, St. Mary's Hospital

Life Beyond Time Management

How High Achievers Balance and Succeed in a Rapidly Changing World

Kim Norup

Willy Norup

Geodex International, Inc.
Sonoma, California

LIFE BEYOND TIME MANAGEMENT:
How High Achievers Balance and Succeed in a Rapidly Changing World

Copyright © 1997 by Geodex International, Inc.

Published by Geodex International, Inc.
P.O. Box 279
35 Maple Street
Sonoma, CA 95476
(800) 833-3030
www.geodex.com

ISBN 1-890256-32-3
Library of Congress Catalog No. 97-092885

Publisher's Cataloging in Publication
(Prepared by Quality Books Inc.)

Norup, Kim.
    Life beyond time management : how high achievers balance and succeed in a rapidly changing world / by Kim Norup, Willy Norup.
      p.   cm.
    Includes bibliographical references and index.
    ISBN 1-890256-32-3

    1. Life skills — Handbooks, manuals, etc. 2. Success. 3. Self-help techniques. 4. Time management. I. Norup, Willy. II. Title.

HQ2037.N67 1997   646.7
                                    QB197-40032

Legal Notice

This publication is designed to provide accurate and authoritative information in regard to the subject matter covered. It is sold with the understanding that the publisher is not engaged in rendering accounting, legal, or other professional services. If legal advice or other expert assistance is required, the services of a competent professional should be sought.

The purpose of this book is to educate and entertain. The authors and Geodex International, Inc., shall assume neither liability nor responsibility to any person or entity with respect to any loss or damage caused, or alleged to be caused, directly or indirectly by the information contained in this book. (From a Declaration of Principles jointly adopted by a Committee of the American Bar Association and a Committee of Publishers.)

Any person not wishing to be bound by the above may return this book to the publisher for a refund.

Quantity Discounts

Are available on bulk purchases of this book for corporations, government agencies, colleges and universities, and professional associations.

Custom Versions

Special books, booklets, book excerpts, and other custom-designed items can be created in print or electronic media to fit your individual needs. For more information, contact Geodex International, Special Sales Department at P.O. Box 279, 35 Maple Street, Sonoma, CA 95476, or call (800) 833-3030.

THIS BOOK IS DEDICATED TO:

- Our wives, Andrea and Grete, whose friendship, love, counsel, support, and encouragement are so vital to our success and happiness in life.

- Our 100,000+ high-achieving clients, who through their confidence and patronage have given us the knowledge and experience base from which this book is written. Thank you, and may we continue to be of mutual benefit as we help one another to lead balanced, happy, and successful lives.

- Achievers of all professions who seek balance, happiness, fulfillment, and success in life. This book is for you.

Contents

Contents

Preface

SINCE 1962 IT HAS BEEN OUR BUSINESS to help people manage their time and face life's challenges in a logical, organized manner. While our engineering and business training helped us, our creative direction was often shaped as we recognized products or services we needed in our own lives. Most recently, we recognized the need for a life-planning process.

This came about when Willy, at the age of 60, identified the personal need for a systematic retirement planning tool. When he realized that such a tool didn't exist, he began to develop one for his own use. However, as business partners, we quickly realized that we had developed a process that others could use and benefit from, too.

Our life management system was originally intended as a supplement to the personal and business-oriented time management system that was the mainstay of our family business. However, a turning point in our development efforts occurred when we came to four important realizations:

1. Retirement planning is nothing more than planning for a life dominated by the new circumstance of no longer working full time.

2. In principle, retirement planning is the same as planning for any new stage in life, and this is something all of us should do as we mature.

3. Success and true happiness in a rapidly changing world are entirely a function of periodically finding a new and acceptable balance in life.

4. Improving time management skills is useless if we spend our time on the wrong things in life. Therefore there is an urgent need for defining life beyond time management.

These four realizations pointed us toward a very important conclusion: You can't start planning your life soon enough. Planning for retirement should begin at the age of 20, as just one of the components of life planning. And from an ongoing process of long-term planning, not only can you reach your goals for retirement but you can focus on reaching your goals and achieving success during all the stages of your life.

In our own lives, we have learned that maintaining a balance between professional and personal life is the key to success and happiness. We've also learned that to succeed in our chosen endeavors it is necessary to recognize and embrace the enormous changes taking place in the world as well as within ourselves. We have no control over many of the changes happening around us, but we can control how we work them into our life plan. Similarly, although we cannot control everything that happens within ourselves, we can learn to accept and adjust to those developments. In the final analysis, we have absolute control over only one thing: the choices we make.

In this book, we present to you the techniques and tools you'll need to take charge of your life, a life beyond time management, and make it the best it can be in our rapidly changing world.

Kim Norup   **Willy Norup**

Sonoma, California
February 1997

Acknowledgments

WE GRATEFULLY ACKOWLEDGE and thank the following people:

Grete Norup, whose intellectual curiosity and logical reasoning helped us to stay on track. Without her nothing would be possible, and with her everything is.

John Williams, the maverick Aussie whose "down under" perspective made us see ourselves and our products in a new light. His enthusiasm when playing in our sandbox resulted in breakthroughs and revelations too numerous to mention.

Terri Lonier, whose ideas, editorial comments, and contagious enthusiasm inspired us to self-publish.

John Baucom, Ph.D., for his numerous content and stylistic comments, as well as the balance test.

Rev. Richard Gantenbein, who lent the perspective of his many years preaching experience to remind us about walking in the reader's shoes and seeing the world through the reader's eyes.

Peter Drucker, in our opinion the most influential management theorist of all time. His teaching provides the philosophical base for much of our work.

Harry Swift, an early mentor for Willy who, although long deceased, still has a powerful influence. His legacy lives on in the spirit of this work.

Dan Poynter, whose vast experience and sage counsel has helped so many authors publish and market their own books.

Lorna Cunkle, who masterfully pulled our manuscript together and helped us deliver the final product you now hold in your hands.

CHAPTER 1

The Challenge

Life belongs to the living, and he who lives must be prepared for changes.
— Johann von Goethe[1]

THE ONLY CONSTANT IN LIFE IS CHANGE. The bad news for people whose goal in life is to achieve stability is that the world is changing at an unprecedented rate. A state of permanence is simply no longer possible. This change in our lives is much like rowing a boat on a river; the faster the water flows downstream, the more futile any attempt to row upstream will become. Many people are so busy reacting to change — furiously trying to row upstream — that their days are filled with stress, worry, and failure.

The good news is that it's possible to take control of your life. This book will show you how. Some people are successful in handling the changes forced upon them by circumstances or their own advancing age, but many are so busy dealing with change that they have no time left to make plans for their life. The ongoing challenge is to react positively and proactively to the many opportunities presented by change. This means making plans, being prepared to embrace change, and choosing to pursue your goals in spite of constant change.

Universal Forces That Drive Change

The world hates change, yet it is the only thing that has brought progress.
— Charles F. Kettering[2]

The United Nations estimates that the world population reached 5.8 billion in 1996, and is increasing annually by more than 90 million.[3] The current rate of growth, 1.4 percent per year, is the direct result of two centuries of advances in scientific knowledge, agriculture, and medicine. More recently, in the past four decades a new phase of population growth was ushered in when famine and disease, especially in underdeveloped areas of the world, could be easily controlled by vaccines, antibiotics, insecticides, and high-yielding varieties of seeds.

Also contributing to this population growth is the fact that the average life expectancy is increasing. Those born in 1950 could expect to live 35 to 40 years (this is a worldwide average). By 1995 life expectancy had increased to 66 years. This trend is expected to continue at a rate of two years each decade.

This truly amazing growth in the world's population will continue to create more crowded living conditions, especially in urban areas. In 1950, 20 percent of the world population was living in urban areas, but by the year 2000 this figure is expected to be 50 percent. The United States covers an area of 5.4 million square miles, yet 97 percent of the population resides on just 3 percent of the land mass. Fully half of our population lives within 50 miles of the Atlantic or Pacific Ocean. These more densely packed urban areas have predictably ushered in a number of modern realities: increasing traffic congestion, growing pollution of air and water, and a higher rate of crime.

The growing population is obviously a large factor that propels change, but many other key change agents are at work in our tumultuous world. On a day-by-day basis, each one may be small and perhaps imperceptible, but their cumulative effect is enormous.

Worldwide Economic Forces

The economic environment of countries all over the world has been changing rapidly and at an increasing speed. Since the end of the Cold War, there has been a significant shift of resources away from the defense industry. The U.S. military and the Defense Department are operating with half a million fewer people, and that trend is worldwide. The determination of our elected officials to wrestle with the budget deficit is also having worldwide repercussions.

Underdeveloped countries are becoming industrial market economies. People living under totalitarian regimes are throwing out dictators or experimenting with free enterprise. A new global marketplace is emerging. This international competition drives businesses to improve quality while cutting prices.

In highly developed countries like the United States, private businesses and government agencies are reacting by merging, reengineering, downsizing, and rightsizing. A new statistic now appears along with unemployment figures: jobs that have been eliminated. The Bureau of Labor Statistics measures the ratio of permanently terminated workers to temporarily laid-off employees. During the last three recessions, that figure has been 1.5 to 1 (1975), 2 to 1 (1982), and 4 to 1 (1993). This means that by now only one of every four laid-off workers will be rehired.

The message is clear, explains William Bridges in *Job Shift:* "Jobs are going away, not just until times improve but for good."[4] Though jobs may be going away, work is not. Manpower, a temporary employment agency, has more than half a million employees, making it the largest private employer in the United States. Temporary and part-time workers are now a vital part of the workforce in all professions. Add to that the growing number of

3

self-employed — professionals, technicians, subcontractors, consultants, and freelancers — and you see a significant shift in work patterns.

Michael Hammer, author of *Reengineering the Corporation,* describes how each person has become both a producer and a consumer.[5] The same worker who wants to do less for more is also a consumer who wants to *pay* less for more. This example dramatically represents the real dichotomy in our society: We want more, yet we aren't willing to work harder for it. This alone shows that we haven't come to grips with the pervasive and worldwide changes in the global economy.

Cultural and Social Forces

Immigration across borders and movement within countries are now becoming commonplace. As workers become more mobile with skills that are more transferable, the tightly knit family and village structures are dissolving. Traditional lifestyles and family values are crumbling. The barriers between ethnic groups, religions, regions, and countries are becoming less important. The same clothes, food, cars, and electronic equipment are becoming abundantly available worldwide. Young people are exposed to and sometimes adopting religious and moral values that are different from those of their parents.

The rate of divorce has doubled in the past twenty years. In the United States, 55 percent of all marriages end in divorce. Marriages are no longer considered a necessity for living together and having children. Same-sex marriages, interracial marriages, and single-parent families are common. Even though fertility is declining worldwide, the burden of raising children has increased as families become smaller and increasing numbers of single parents function without an extended family support system.[6]

Generations no longer live together in the same house, or even in the same community or country. Less than one-fourth of

American households fit the traditional model of a mother and father living with their children. And families suffering under the strains of these changes fail to find support in the resources available through dwindling government funding.

Throughout the world governments are struggling to provide the social services needed or expected by their citizens. The age of entitlement seems to be drawing to a close. At the same time, a greater disparity is emerging between the rich and poor, with substantial financial uncertainly among both groups. The age of self-security is replacing the age of social-security as more and more people are being forced to make a dramatic shift toward taking responsibility for retirement income and health care.

Technological Forces

Six billion people worldwide consume enormous amounts of products and services, but they also fuel the development of new technology. New technologies — not just new products — are introduced and penetrate the culture in what seems like the blink of an eye. And that pace of innovation shows no sign of declining. We've been turning jobs over to machines for more than a hundred years. We are now at the point where we are producing five times more than we were even fifty years ago with the same number of workers.

More than 80 percent of the world's technological advances have occurred since 1900, yet they're also becoming obsolete at a faster rate than ever before. Predictions indicate that technological growth in the last fifteen years of the twentieth century will equal that of the first eighty-five years. Within some fields of high technology, "state-of-the-art" becomes "obsolete" in less than a year, and as technology advances, people must learn to adapt.

Technological changes are an appropriate yardstick for measuring change because the advancement of technology is behind many of the changes in our personal lives. Witness the dramatic changes in communications technology (telephone answering machine, fax machine, cellular phone, e-mail, Internet), home electronics (television, personal computer, video recorder, compact disc player, remote control, laptop and hand-held computers) and even automotive engineering (air bags, antilock brakes, electronic fuel injection). These changes are affecting the way we live, work, and play every single day, and they suggest that flexibility is an important trait for survival.

Growth of Information as a Commodity

The invention of new products does not totally explain the profound nature of the changes we are seeing as we enter the twenty-first century. In the production cycle, workers used to fill out papers every step along the way. Now information moves electronically through the cycle of production — from purchasing to suppliers of raw materials (perhaps in different locations or different companies) to the receiving dock to the factory to the accounting department to the sales outlet. In the end, the number of workers needed to produce any given product is drastically reduced, and the production cycle becomes faster and more efficient.

We are now at the point where more than one-third of American employees work with information rather than products. According to figures from the 1990 U.S. Census and the Department of Labor, more Americans work in the computer industry than in the auto, steel, mining, and oil industries combined. And the U.S. Department of Labor estimates that by the year 2000 at least 44 percent of all workers will be in data services — gathering, processing, retrieving, or analyzing information.

Fueled by technology, the amount of information available to us is doubling every five years. More information was generated in the thirty-year period between 1966 and 1996 than in the previous five thousand years. Communications technology no longer allows us to ignore the political situation in the Middle East, the

6

famine in Africa, the population explosion in India, or the newest software startup company in Silicon Valley. Change has always occurred, but now we are instantaneously aware of it. In our society it is becoming very difficult to live in ignorant bliss.

This rapid growth and proliferation of information is reshaping the workplace. The procedures of the age of industrialism are too slow and too rigid for a world networked by electronic data. This easily accessible information has also brought about a redistribution of power.

In the industrial age, workers had to live near where they worked while power was in the hands of only a few business owners. In the technological age, more and more people are taking hold of the power to make meaningful choices in their lives, especially related to where they live and where they work. "The age of industry was fueled by the mining of finite natural resources," writes Richard Saul Wurman in *Information Anxiety.* "Information is infinite and cannot be treated as a tangible product. It is harder to define, to control, to predict, but its potential is boundless."[7]

Managing the growing availability of information affects more than the working hours of any given day. The process of learning how to find what we need from the ocean of information available to us is somewhat overwhelming. We are constantly bombarded with newspapers, television programming, magazines, billboards, Internet resources, music, movies, videotapes, books, and books on tapes. A wise information consumer realizes that it is impossible to read (or view) and absorb even a small portion of the information that is available to us. Being selective becomes essential for success, even survival.

How Change Affects Individuals

We are restless because of incessant change, but we would be frightened if change were stopped.
— Lyman Lloyd Bryson[8]

Thirty years ago, the futurist Alvin Toffler predicted that we would eventually be overwhelmed by too many choices. He named this modern dilemma "future shock" and defined it as "...the shattering stress and disorientation that we induce in individuals by subjecting them to too much change in too short a time."[9] He wrote that this would inhibit action, produce a higher level of anxiety, and foster the perception that both freedom and time are becoming scarce. The rapid changes we face daily seem to fulfill this prediction.

Whether foreseeable or totally unexpected, change tends to create confusion and turmoil. Increasing competition, a more hectic pace of activity, and information overload all contribute to an extremely high level of stress. *Too often, the result is an overwhelming feeling of being out of control, yet desperately trying to regain control tends to obscure the perspective necessary for success and happiness.*

Even if the political, economic, and social environment remained constant, people would still experience change as they pass through various stages of life. In the modern world, these normal and fairly predictable life changes are played out against a backdrop of an accelerating rate of change in the world. In both the corporate and government worlds, downsizing and reengineering have become common practice. Many of the castoffs from this movement are being thrown into a competitive job market with little or no warning. Shifting roles at work and at home bring new responsibilities and a sense of imbalance — the feeling that life is unmanageable or out of control. Much in our culture (from

Hollywood to fashions) popularizes youth and thereby conflicts with the inevitability of the changes resulting from getting older. All this can quickly develop into feelings of futility and despair. No wonder depression is becoming so pervasive in our rapidly evolving world.

Embrace Change

Although you have no control over the universal forces that bring about change, *you do have control over how you respond.* You can dig in your heels and resist the winds of change, or you can pause to observe, measure, and then change course. Although, difficult and sometimes painful personal decisions are part of the process, our experience has shown that the key to success is to create a life plan that is flexible and responsive to circumstances while maintaining stable relationships within the work and home environments.

To get a secure handle on the many ways that change affects individuals, we have found it helpful to look at modern-day life as basically comprised of three areas of activities: work, self, and home. For the purposes of this book, we define these spheres of influence as follows:

 Your professional career. Those activities for which you are compensated. Ideally, work is also psychologically rewarding.

 Your inner being. Your mental, physical, spiritual, and emotional growth and well-being.

 Everything else in your life, including your family, friends, and community.

Like the legs of a three-legged stool, the three spheres of influence are all needed for stability. All three are important facets of life, and one sphere is not necessarily more important

Figure 1.1
Three spheres of influence in modern-day life:
work, self, and home

than another. Research and our experience with more than
100,000 clients reinforce what common sense tells us: *Ignore
any one of the spheres of influence and the result is a life out
of balance, along with accompanying feelings of stress, guilt,
and unhappiness.*

Just as life circumstances change with time, the three
spheres of influence change in size and in relation to each other.
Each person chooses to balance the three spheres of influence in
a way that is unique and that changes over time. At times, the
focus may be on work, while at other times family responsibilities
may be the highest priority. For example, the work sphere of
influence will typically be very small or perhaps nonexistent for
an adolescent, whereas for the typical middle-aged adult work
will assume a much greater significance until retirement.

Much like the decorative pieces on a mobile, the three
spheres of influence can be in balance in a myriad of positions.
Time passes. Circumstances change. Crises occur. Life easily gets
too complicated when the responsibilities of the three spheres of
influence place conflicting demands on you. The trick is to maintain balance no matter how hard the wind blows, and that balance
is often maintained by adapting to the changing wind.

*When these key areas of your life are out of balance, you
will feel increasing amounts of psychological stress. You may
become depressed or extremely nervous. You will lose your*

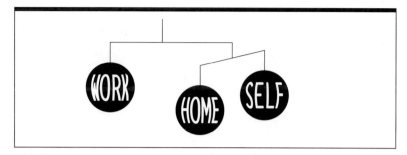

Figure 1.2
Balancing the three spheres of influence: the mobile

focus, your productivity will fall, your goals will seem impossible to achieve. Success and happiness will seem far removed and impossible to reach.

The challenge to maintain a satisfactory balance seems to grow greater as we age and gradually raise our level of effort and involvement in the three spheres of influence. Perhaps you've noticed that life seems to become progressively more busy and more challenging with each passing year — clearly the result of increased responsibility and involvement in all three spheres. Balance is the crucial ingredient to creating success and preserving your sanity.

When one sphere of your life is not going well, it often has an adverse effect on one or both of the other spheres, thereby throwing your life out of balance. Examples of this have happened to all of us at one time or another:

- An argument at the breakfast table with your spouse can (and typically will) run your business day.
- Not feeling well physically quickly affects your mental outlook on life.
- A bad day at the office may ruin the evening with your family.

- A tough commute through bad weather or worse-than-usual traffic may put you in a bad mood and thereby affect your treatment of coworkers or family members.
- A financial problem or a business mistake will have a negative effect on your self-esteem.

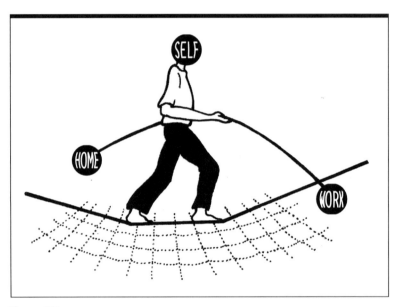

Figure 1.3
Balancing the three spheres of influence: the tightrope walker

Much as the keel helps to stabilize a boat and keep it on course, balance provides the strength, stability, and direction needed to maintain health and happiness in your life. The art of tightrope walking provides another metaphor for balancing work, self, and home. Consider work and home at opposite of ends of the tightrope walker's balancing pole, with self in the middle.

The balancing pole provides stability, while the safety net ensures that mistakes are not fatal. Movement makes stability easier — the tightrope walker moves constantly while making literally hundreds of minor balance adjustments and corrections every minute. Similarly, it is easier to maintain balance if you're moving forward toward clearly defined goals, and the adjustments needed to maintain balance are relatively small and easy to execute while you are moving forward.

To continue the tightrope walker metaphor, the pole can be seen as a tool that allows balance to be maintained when the spheres of influence change in size. A life plan, family, friends, and inner strength become the secure safety net that accommodates the taking of risks or experimentation with contingency plans. Any movement toward a clearly defined goal contributes to stability and makes adjustments necessitated by changing circumstances easy to implement.

On pages 14 and 15 you'll find a summary of how change affects the three spheres of influence. When we look closely at the universal forces of change and how they impact individuals, we can see that two different types of events force us into a position where we need to make a personal decision:

- Events that are predictable and controllable (for example, sending a child to college, retiring from the workforce).

- Random, unpredictable events (for example, suddenly deciding to switch careers, receiving a promotion that requires moving 2000 miles, losing a job, getting a divorce).

Change in the Three Spheres of Influence

- Increase in ranks of the unemployed and the early retired as goods and services are produced by fewer people and the world's population grows.
- Disappearance of numerous careers and career tracks, emergence of new professions.
- Loss of loyalty to the employer, increase in workplace crime.
- Increase in number of temporary workers, self-employed workers, and small businesses.
- Reallocation of some business functions from one regional area, state, or nation to another.
- Increase in import/export opportunities and growing need for tolerance of those of different racial, ethnic, and national origin as a global marketplace emerges.
- Increase in demand for competent (and increasingly multilingual) communication skills.
- Increasing demand for computer literacy and technical skills, forcing those unwilling to retrain out of the workforce.

- Lack of time to develop personal interests.
- Increasing need to develop transferable skills as old skills become obsolete.
- Increasing stress with growing awareness that job security is tenuous and retirement is not secure.

- Longer periods of unemployment due to more frequent job changes.
- Increase in health problems from growing levels of pollution, pervasiveness of electronics, and repetitive nature of work.
- Guilt over lack of time to participate in social activities with family and community as work obligations and commuting time increase.
- Increasing exploration of and transference to other religions as exposure to other cultures and value systems increases.
- Increasing isolation and decreasing development of social skills as growing percentage of communication is electronic.
- Decrease in number of positive role models or traditional heroes.
- Loss of support of the extended family structure.

- Questioning of traditional definitions or concepts of family as rate of divorce increases and more couples live together without being married.
- Childbearing and childrearing increasingly postponed until the thirties and forties, with fewer children in each family.
- Loss of family cohesion and quality time together in two-career households.
- Less personal interaction as television and computer consume family time.
- Increase in number of home-based workers.
- Worldwide consumer habits replacing national, regional, and familial preferences.
- Increasing numbers of people caring for both children and aging relatives, more adult children choosing to live at home.

Predictable Events

Everyone ages, everyone changes, but most of us follow a fairly predictable path through life. Being aware of where you are in this predictable life cycle and what comes next helps to ease the transition from one stage of life to another. The movement through time leads to changes that you can predict and therefore control. Having a plan helps you maintain equilibrium during the very predictable periods of transition.

Usually, but not always. Predictable events can lead to what we call self-inflicted change. Generally this occurs when you reach a "trigger point" where the pain of not changing is greater than the pain of making a change. Events such as quitting a job, leaving your family, taking an early retirement, or embarking on a rigorous exercise regime generally occur when a breaking point (a "trigger") is reached. Sometimes an opportunity appears, seemingly out of nowhere, that is just too good to pass up. For some compelling reason it becomes clear that to follow the same daily routine as before would cause too much stress and turmoil.

The work-family conflict often results in self-inflicted change, as shown by recent decisions of numerous high-powered executives to cut back on the work commitment as family responsibilities grow. The all-or-nothing demands of many jobs create high amounts of stress for those who also want to be involved in the rearing of their children. (For two case studies, see the boxes on pages 18–21.) Rocky Rhodes, chief engineer at Silicon Graphics, achieved balance by cutting back to part-time work. Trudy DeSilets, a senior manager at Eddie Bauer, resolved the work-family conflict when she found an employer who was committed to the support of family values.

Typical High-Impact Life-Changing Events Within Your Control

- Job skills becoming obsolete.
- Switching to a new career.
- Becoming self-employed or starting a business.

- Returning to school.
- Retiring early.
- Adopting new values.

- Moving to another city or country.
- Adopting an alternative lifestyle.
- Marrying (or remarrying).
- Becoming a parent (or starting a second family).
- Caring for an elderly parent.

Rocky Rhodes
Chief Engineer, Silicon Graphics
Mountain View, California

By the time he was 40, Rocky Rhodes was a success. As a cofounder and chief engineer at Silicon Graphics, he worked on cutting-edge projects. "It was the first time in my life that I was passionate about something," he told us in a recent phone interview. "I really devoted myself to my work and I was surprised at how hard I worked. I never looked at a clock."

Rhodes worked seven days a week, day and night, creating three-dimensional graphics software for the company's workstations. Rhodes' wife, an Apple Computer product manager, was equally immersed in her work. But the birth of their first child, followed by two more in the next four years, has changed everything.

Family responsibilities beckoned and the Rhodes parents struggled to meet them. One day, they hastily scribbled on a yellow Post-It note the four priorities — in order of importance — they agreed were the most important:

1. God
2. Family
3. Exercise
4. Work

Translating these priorities into daily life wasn't easy. Rhodes describes his life during this time as a constant battle. "I tried for a number of years to distance myself from the heart of the frenzy. I wanted to be involved as a major player but I didn't want to work nights and weekends. I tried doing it step by step but it just didn't seem to work for me."

Rhodes had so much trouble trying to cut back that he finally decided to take off the entire summer of 1992, going "cold turkey." Since then, after a few relapses into being fully consumed by product deadlines, he has established a fairly stable balance that is secured by his childcare duties in the morning (he's responsible for getting the kids off to school in the morning), his volunteer work with his church (every Thursday he works with a group on video editing), and the pleasure he gets from spending time alone with his four-year-old son. Exercise is scheduled, too. Twice a week he works out with his wife, twice a week he runs with his buddies from Silicon Graphics, and Saturday morning he runs by himself.

The first three items on the Post-It are easily met, but work is still a struggle. He received a great sense of accomplishment from working closely with a team on product development, yet Rhodes is quick

> *The mechanics of keeping priorities and activities in their proper perspective comes down to two calendars: Mom's and Dad's.*

to describe one of the corresponding benefits of going part-time. When he was absorbed in his work, he would go home and find himself doing something that required no brain power — like watch a movie or read a mystery. Now that he's not mentally exhausted at the end of the day, he finds himself deep into a reading program that includes economics, biology, physics, new technology.

E-mail helps Rhodes stay in touch with the company on days he doesn't go into the office, but it's had an even more profound effect on his personal life. "When I was working so hard I just didn't have time for friends," he explains, "and now e-mail is allowing me to keep in close touch with some people who are important in my life."

The mechanics of keeping priorities and activities in their proper perspective comes down to two calendars: Mom's and Dad's. "It's all written on a calendar," Rhodes explains, "but flexibility is really important, too. If something comes up, I can't just assume my wife will take over. And the best part is that the little hiccups in the schedule, like when a child gets sick, are no longer major crises because of the flexibility my wife and I have worked into our schedules."

Trudy DeSilets

Senior Manager
Marketing Systems & New Customer Acquisitions
Eddie Bauer
Redmond, Washington

Trudy DeSilets has spent much of her adult life searching for an employer who would allow her to meet both personal and professional goals. The first step, a dramatic one, came when her daughter was three years old. DeSilets was doing well in a fast-track sales job, but travel demands and the work-family conflict left her exhausted and under constant stress. Her request for job-sharing was turned down, so she resigned.

This was a very difficult time for DeSilets. She loved her job and she was a well-respected employee. She calls this a wrenching decision because she was unsure of how it would affect her career. She also felt she should have been able to resolve the work-family conflict without having to make a choice.

Since this first step, this irrevocable choice, DeSilets has worked as a consultant, started her own marketing firm, worked as a teacher, and gone back to school to get her M.B.A. She has also been available in the afternoons to be the mother she wanted to be. By the time she joined Eddie Bauer three years ago, she knew she wanted to work for a company where family values are recognized.

The key to resolving the work-family conflict, according to DeSilets, is focusing on your goals. "You have to know what you want and then the rest is a lot easier," she told us. "I was 42 when I got my M.B.A. degree. When I was 37, I wrote down the goals I wanted to achieve and the first one on my list was to go back to graduate school. Then I wrote down all the steps I needed to take. I even had a friend support me. She would call and check on my progress."

This was the first time DeSilets did something specifically for herself. Before that things just sort of happened to her. "My husband and

I had set goals in our personal life that were related to savings or travel or retirement, but this time I focused on myself," she says. With some clarity about her work-related goals, she found it easier to stand by her values. Before joining Eddie Bauer, she worked a short time for an employer who not only refused to allow her time off for a religious holiday but would not even acknowledge that this was important to her and her family. DeSilets resigned, and this time it wasn't difficult.

To keep track of her various commitments, DeSilets maintains one master calendar for work, home, and exercise. She keeps her husband's schedule on this calendar, too. Then if both he and her daughter have evening plans, she has the option to plan an extra game of tennis or catch up on some work projects.

Since she began working for Eddie Bauer, DeSilets has an added commitment to exercise. "I think physical fitness helps your mental ability, helps you handle the stress better," she says. Eddie Bauer supports physical exercise, too, with an on-site workout facility, and DeSilets schedules two tennis games a week, too.

Family issues are part of Eddie Bauer's strategic business plan, and not just in words on paper. Corporate headquarters includes a lactation room for nursing mothers, a cafeteria that cooks up take-home dinners for late-working employees, and a paid "balance day" that lets workers take time off for things like parent-teacher conferences. Flexible hours allow some employees to work 6:30 to 3:30, and during the summer four long workdays can be scheduled, which allows for extended weekends. It's no wonder the company has received several awards for their progressive attitude. Most recently, *Business Week* named Eddie Bauer one of the country's top ten family-friendly companies.

"Now I'm working with some women who have young children," DeSilets explains, "and I'm happy that Eddie Bauer is so very supportive of working out flexible shifts for them. It makes the job a lot easier."

Unpredictable Events

Sooner or later, most of us face a seemingly random event imposed by circumstances beyond our control. In addition, we make numerous decisions throughout our life that are not predictable because they do not fit into any pattern. These are uncontrollable changes you can't predict, but you must deal with them as they occur before you can get on with your life.

**Unpredictable Events
in the Three Spheres of Influence**

- Losing a job (laid off or fired).
- Being required to embrace technological advancements.
- Restructuring due to political or economic crises.

- Psychological crisis.
- Religious conversion.
- Serious health problems.

- Unexpected financial setback.
- Divorce.
- Death of spouse, child, parent, or close friend.
- Natural or man-made catastrophes such as fire, earthquake, hurricane, flood, or war.

Sometimes one of these unforeseen events is so traumatic it is called a crisis. At other times, these events can be overwhelmingly wonderful — being honored with the Nobel Prize, for example, or receiving a prestigious political appointment. In either case, the changes that are brought by unforeseen events affect all three spheres of influence.

Accommodating Change

God,
Grant me:
Serenity to accept the things I cannot change,
Courage to change the things I can,
And the wisdom to know the difference.
— Serenity Prayer[10]

When combined with the universal forces that drive change, personal changes — whether predictable or not — can create a tremendous amount of stress, turmoil, and confusion on a daily basis. Those who are most successful at adapting to the forces of change are those who quickly refocus their outlook and rebalance their spheres of influence.

Some changes sneak up on you gradually. If you watch for them and keep an open mind, you can easily navigate around them or even take advantage of the waves they create. As you'll see in subsequent chapters of this book, you can make a life plan for accommodating and living comfortably with most of the predictable changes that develop gradually.

Other changes will hit you like a bolt of lightning coming out of a clear blue sky. You never see them coming. (See pages 24–25 for an example of how one person, actor Christopher Reeve, responded to unpredictable change.) And when the unexpected

Continued on page 26

Christopher Reeve
Actor and Political Activist

On Memorial Day in 1995, Christopher Reeve's life was tragically and irrevocably altered. He was thrown from a horse during a riding competition and since that moment he has been paralyzed from the neck down. Although Reeve's prognosis is poor, his progress is amazing. In the fifteen months since the accident, he has learned to shrug his shoulders and breathe on his own for lengthening periods of time.

Until the unforeseen tragedy, Reeve had been a successful actor, thrown into the lap of success with his portrayal of Superman in 1978. He was also married, the father of three children, and a political activist. He had testified before Congress on behalf of educational funding, and he was an outspoken supporter of Save the Children and Amnesty International.

Within three months of his accident, Reeve began a dedicated crusade to increase the public's awareness of the 250,000 Americans who live with paralysis. Most are young men, injured in automobile accidents. Ninety percent survive, only to live an average of 40 years in wheelchairs.

Reeve continues to lobby for legislation that will prevent insurance companies from setting lifetime caps on compensation for spinal-cord injuries and that will increase spending on research. He suggests that $40 million a year for the next ten years could help him and others leave their wheelchairs, saving billions now spent on long-term care.

The extent of Reeve's success is already immense. A California philanthropist donated $1 million for the establishment of a research center at the University of California in Irvine and the California legislature has pledged matching funds. But Reeve's personal method for overcoming adversity must be applauded as well. In recent interviews with both *Time* and *Newsweek,* he spoke openly of his need to turn the crisis into something meaningful.[11]

Reeve is described as living between the acceptance of the reality of his condition and the expectation of changing it. He has accepted the fact that the central nervous system does not regenerate the way the peripheral system does. He acknowledges struggling with feelings of self-pity and describes the realization that the question for him is no longer "What life do I have?" but "What life can I build?"

"And the answer, surprisingly, is 'More than you think,'" he told *Newsweek.* He began to see that he could use his popularity to lead a

---

Christopher Reeve doesn't go so far as to admit that there was a reason for the accident, but he has seized the opportunity to make sense of it.

---

movement, that he could use relationships already in place with legislators to raise funds for a cure. Awareness of spinal-cord injury is at an all-time high. People now understand that what was thought incurable is not necessarily true. The politicians are motivated, the scientists are motivated.

Christopher Reeve doesn't go so far as to admit that there was a reason for the accident, but he has seized the opportunity to make sense of it. A common reference in Reeve's speeches is to John Kennedy's promise that by the end of the 1960s there would be an American on the moon. He likes to point out that everybody, including the scientists, shook their heads in disbelief.

"I believe it's what you do after a disaster that gives it meaning," he told *Time.* "When Kennedy made that promise, I mean … what chutzpa to do that! Promise to do what other people say is impossible. I guess that's what leadership is. What's the adage? 'Give me a place to stand, and I can move the world'? Well, I'm not comparing myself to the world's leaders. And I can't stand yet. But give me a place to sit…."[12]

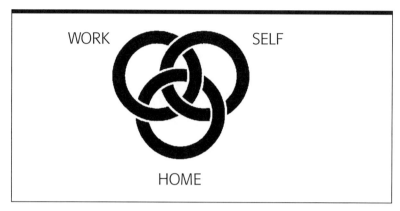

Figure 1.4
Following a lifestage plan can help you keep the three spheres
of influence in balance

happens, you may be forced to make a sudden revision of your
plans. In principle, you deal with these unforeseen changes the
same way you deal with the predictable changes, but here you
have no warning. Having a plan will keep you from floundering.

Any changes you decide to make, or are forced to make by
unforeseen circumstances, will affect all three spheres of influence. You only have a limited amount of time, energy, and
resources. The unexpected or unusual demand from one sphere
of life will be met by taking from another, and this give-and-take
adjustment will naturally create a new balance for your life.

Happily Ever After

Happiness is mostly a by-product of doing what makes us feel fulfilled.
-- Dr. Benjamin Spock[13]

Happiness is difficult to define and even more difficult to achieve. One look at a healthy baby will confirm that humans have a natural predisposition toward happiness. True happiness and success are as natural as absolute silence or perfect balance. But what happens as we go through life? Why do so many people find happiness to be so elusive? Part of the problem is that most people have never taken the time to figure out exactly what happiness or success looks like in their life.

Society tends to use high income and wealth as indicators of success, probably because money is a convenient measurement and easier to quantify than happiness. The prevailing conclusion is that if you have a high income or are wealthy, then you are successful and, by logical extension, happy as well.

Yet seldom are the wealthiest people also the happiest. As noted motivational speaker Zig Ziglar once observed, "Money can buy you a house, but not a home; a good bed, but not a good night's sleep; a companion, but not a friend."[14] The Beatles, rich and famous, sang, "Money can't buy me love."[15] Money can buy many things, but it can't buy friendship, peace of mind, or happiness, either.

Happiness is largely a function of how well your life is in balance and whether or not you feel like you are making progress toward your personal definition of success. Sure, it is difficult to maintain balance during periods of crisis or change, and this is the root of the problem for many people. Can the three spheres of influence be permanently kept in balance? Probably not, considering how rapidly our world is changing. But it is possible to quickly rebalance your life and get on with living it to the fullest.

Exercise
The Success Trap

The first and single most important step to take toward achieving success is to define what success means to you. To the casual observer, many high achievers have realized a high level of success, yet when asked they often admit that they don't feel successful at all. Why? They have fallen into the success trap. They have never bothered to establish what success means within the scope of their own life.

Without a clear definition of success, very few people will know when they've achieved it. Without a clear definition of success, many people are forever chasing after the next rainbow instead of celebrating their achievements. This common trap can tarnish your enthusiasm for life and steal away your motivation. Take a few moments to reflect upon what success means to you.

Life as Seen from a Helicopter

To begin the life-balancing process, you need to have an overview of your life. For this task, we strongly recommend the use of a helicopter, the amazing flying machine that allows its pilot to travel in all directions, to hover up high or to swoop down for a closer look. You can use a helicopter to identify the major components of your life and to begin to see how they interrelate.

You won't need gasoline on this journey, for the helicopters we advocate are fueled by thought. We recommend a "mental" helicopter: a thinking device that will allow you to see the territory you have already covered, where you are now, and what's coming up ahead.

Figure 1.5
Using a mental helicopter, you can get an overview of where you are
and where you are going

Your mental helicopter could be a sailboat, a mountain bike, a
pair of hiking boots, a bathtub, or a "Do Not Disturb" sign on your
office door. Once you experience the power of your helicopter,
it'll likely become one of your most prized possessions.

Exercise
Helicopter Pilot's Instructions

You can fly your helicopter anywhere: at the office, in the car, at home, even on vacation. Your personal helicopter is as portable as you are. Follow these simple instructions:

1. Find a quiet time and place, somewhere you can be alone without any interruptions. You can fly outdoors (your backyard, a park, a nearby wilderness area) or in any room where you can be alone and undisturbed.

2. Set aside at least ten to twenty minutes for a decent flight.

3. Be prepared to capture any thoughts, revelations or obstacles you observe. Bring with you paper and pen or a tape recorder. Quickly record them and resume flying.

4. Don't be afraid to take a chance. Venture out into uncharted territory by playing mental "what-if" games. This is one aircraft you cannot possibly crash, so let your inhibitions go. Chase your impulses and intuition! You might be surprised where this will lead you.

5. For your first flight, go straight up and get an overview of your life! As you fly higher, you will begin to see your life in perspective. You see all the demands and opportunities, the changes, risks, and rewards in your life. Notice how different things look from a distance. Little irritants become almost invisible and the really important things in life stand out. With this overview you can begin to see what is going on, what to do, what to change, and what can or should be ignored for now.

This should not be a one-time flight. Adopt the habit of taking a weekly helicopter trip, a quiet ten minutes to take an overview of your life and plan for the most meaningful next steps. Recharge your mental batteries and make sure that you are on track to be the best that you can be.

Planning for Success

*If one advances confidently in the direction of his dreams,
and endeavors to live the life which he has imagined, he
will meet with a success unexpected in common hours.*
— Henry David Thoreau[16]

Life presents the same basic choice, over and over again: *Accept things as they are or take responsibility for making changes.* Seize the day or let outside events forge your destiny. Approach the future's unforeseeable changes as a source of opportunity or a trigger for anxiety. The quality of life, day after day, is the direct result of this basic choice.

The level of enjoyment any given person experiences on the journey through life is directly related to the development of plans and the making of conscious choices. In the end, responding to change with a positive attitude and in a proactive manner allows ever-changing circumstances to become unforeseen opportunities.

The systematic and logical approach to life planning that is presented in the remaining chapters of this book will help you deal with the changes you encounter while you strive to build a meaningful, successful, and happy future. The secret to living a happy and fulfilled life is elusive and differs greatly from person to person. This book will not tell you what you need to do to succeed. Rather, we offer a method for analyzing your life situation and achieving an optimum balance of work, self, and home. Even unexpected crises will be met with a stronger ability to refocus and rebalance your life.

As time passes, you must be prepared to adjust your attitude, your actions, and your plans in order to take advantage of ever-changing circumstances, often without much warning. You must be prepared to review the way you use your time and your resources, as well as how you plan to spend them in the future.

Do not count on a straight path from point A to point B. Rather, be prepared for mid-course corrections in the same way that a sailboat must tack to advance against adverse winds.

Inhibiting forces reside with the self. When you are able to confront your fears and examine your beliefs, then you will be able to embrace change and use it to your advantage. Success in the modern world comes in spite of change, and those who cannot accommodate the shifting tides are doomed to a life of constant stress, worry, and a sense of failure. Invisible forces compel movement, change literally propels evolution. *Change is one of the few constants in the world. Make it your friend.*

The Foundation

The life unexamined is not worth living.
— Plato[1]

VERY FEW PEOPLE SPEND TIME THINKING about what makes them unique or what motivates them. Nor do most people realize that they actually have the power and ability to do what truly makes them feel happy and fulfilled in life. Even those who ponder the meaning of life in an abstract sense may not know how to define, let alone find, the best direction for their own personal life. As you will see in Chapters 2 and 3, this is not a difficult task.

To begin planning for a balanced, successful life, you first need to know your exact location, where you are now in your development. Once your current lifestage has been pinpointed, you need to define your vision, your motivators, and your purpose. These will become the foundation for your lifestage plan and the personal compass that will help you maintain your bearings when the seas of life become rough. (See Figure 2.1 on the following page for an illustration of this process.)

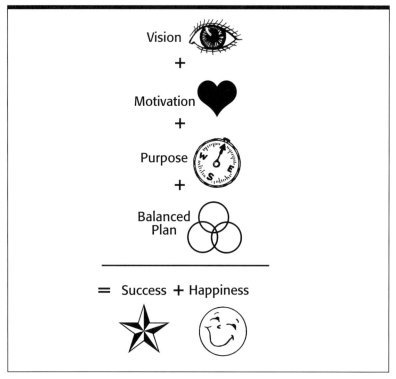

Figure 2.1
Taking charge of your life: the process

Stages of Development

> The greatest thing in this world is not so much where we
> are, but in which direction we are moving.
> — Oliver Wendell Holmes[2]

Life is constantly in transition. Changes are inevitable and they're
not all bad. Between birth and death everyone goes through a
series of relatively stable stages of structure building, renewal,
and fulfillment, with intermittent transition periods. Major events
take place in roughly the same sequence — life moves each per-

son through a typical series of stages with fairly predictable outcomes. With the proper preparation and attitude, this process of maturation can be an enriching and rewarding experience.

The concept of the stages of life following each other in a more or less linear fashion has been the subject of study for years.[3] Many people do follow a typical pattern and for these people the lifestages become valuable guides. But there are exceptions — people who do not follow a common or predictable pattern, for whatever reason. In addition, unpredictable events tend to move people, regardless of their age, either back to a previous stage or forward to a later stage. Nevertheless, knowledge of life's stages is useful as a beginning point for life planning. At the very least, an understanding of the stages of life serves as an excellent resource for ideas on personal actions and directions to take, or to avoid.

Based on our own life experiences plus a synthesis of our research and that done by others, these are the common stages we typically experience are described on the following pages.

Exercise
Where Are You?

Read through the descriptions of the ten lifestages for guidance, ideas, and inspiration. Then place a checkmark next to the descriptions that apply to your present situation (or write them down on a separate sheet of paper). This important groundwork will help you complete the exercises later in this chapter.

Life does not always follow a straight path and the progression through these stages is not always as outlined here. If you find yourself in several different lifestages at this time, do not conclude that you are fragmenting yourself or living a disjointed life. There is no right or wrong. Rather, as you blaze your own trail you demonstrate a wholesome integration of life's possibilities.

The typical age shown for each of the lifestages is an approximate indicator. Biological age and its corresponding lifestage are not always in synchronization. This only points out uniqueness and an ability to adapt. For example, midlife crisis can occur as early as age 35 or as late as 55 — or not at all. Having children at age 40 is not uncommon, and 65 is no longer a mandatory retirement age as many people leave the workforce much earlier or choose to keep working through their seventies and eighties.

Sometimes the passage from one lifestage to another is made during a single event (marriage, birth of a child, retirement), but more often the transition is subtle and even imperceptible except in hindsight. During transition periods, people tend to evaluate the past, redefine the vision of the future, and perhaps change the structure of day-to-day life to bring about improved balance. These are true stress periods when confusion and turmoil reign. Sight of what's important tends to become cloudy. *Balance is often difficult — and sometimes impossible — to attain during periods of transition.*

Childhood (0–16)

Since this book focuses on adults (or those soon to be), an overview of the childhood lifestage is not included.

Youth (16–20)

Duration: 3–5 years

Spheres of influence: focus on SELF

What generally happens:

- Gaining freedom of movement, perhaps with a first car.
- Pulling up roots, seeking adult identity with less dependence on parents.
- Working part-time.
- Leaving high school; entering college or the workforce.

- Looking into career options.
- Seeking many friends, peer approval important.
- Testing capabilities and lifestyle.

Young Adult Transition (20–23)

Duration: 2–5 years

Spheres of influence: focus on SELF while struggling to establish a new balance

What generally happens:

- Evaluating various career paths.
- Pursuing academic studies or developing a career.
- Taking life more seriously, including close friendships.
- Considering where to live.
- Testing relationships and lifestyles.

Emerging Career (23–28)

Duration: 6–8 years

Spheres of influence: focus on WORK

What generally happens:

- Making of serious commitments.
- Beginning of career.
- Working hard, working long hours.
- Forming of close relationships.
- Marriage and establishment of first home
- Birth of first child.
- Life falling into a more settled pattern.
- For some, trouble adjusting to marriage and/or parenting.
- For some, external pressure and internal conflict.
- For some, lifestyle changes.
- Job change(s) common.
- Testing relationships and lifestyles.

Settling Down Transition (28–30)

Duration: 1–2 years

Spheres of influence: focus on WORK, struggling to find a balance

What generally happens:

- Earlier commitments to lifestyle, career, and community may be questioned or affirmed.
- Discovering limitations in abilities and opportunities.
- Becoming aware of the passage of time and the aging process.

Settling Down & Grounding (30–40)

Duration: 8–10 years

Spheres of influence: WORK, SELF, and HOME given equal attention

What generally happens:

- Making long-term commitments to work.
- Career recognition becoming important.
- Firming up relationships.
- Getting married and having children.
- Material success becoming important.
- Trading up to a larger house.
- Life settling into a comfortable pattern.
- For some, upheavals in marriage and lifestyle.
- Working to pay for it all takes time and energy.
- Earlier commitments to lifestyle, career, and may be questioned or affirmed.
- Giving first thoughts to retirement and mortality.

Midlife Transition (40–45)

Duration: 2–5 years

Spheres of influence: confusion, looking for a new balance

What generally happens:

- Confronting the gap between aspirations and reality.
- Questioning of relationships, achievements, and life purpose: What is success? What is life all about? What am I living for? How can I have more fun?

 Stability & Harvesting (45–60+)

Duration: 10–20 years

Spheres of influence: WORK, SELF, and HOME given approximately equal attention

What generally happens:

- Lifestyle settled and stable.
- Children beginning to leave home.
- Importance of family and friends.
- Possibly acquiring a second home.
- Trying out various leisure-time activities, including travel.
- Career (and income) peaks.
- Beginning of serious retirement planning.
- Investments demanding attention.
- Enjoying the "here and now."
- Major disruptions (for example, loss of spouse, close friend, or job) forcing some to return to earlier lifestages.

 Retirement Transition (60–65)

Duration: 1–3 years

Spheres of influence: diminished attention to WORK

What generally happens:

- Short, uncertain period.
- There are fewer demands on time.

- Preparing for a more leisurely lifestyle.
- May no longer have to work for money.
- Realization of some bodily decline.

Post-Retirement (65+)

Duration: as few as 1 year, as many as 25 or 30 years

Spheres of influence: minimal focus on WORK

What generally happens:

- Often a happy and rewarding time.
- Less pressure to get things done, more time to enjoy the little things in life.
- Living in the present.
- Accepting oneself and (barring any health problems) experiencing a gradual relaxation into the wisdom of the elders.
- Challenged to find spiritual peace of mind.
- Retirement, lose of companions, and shifting away from paid work may be traumatic and require major adjustments in attitude and lifestyle.
- More money to spend, enjoying personal comforts.
- Focusing on financial security and estate planning.
- Busy with hobbies, including travel.

Each stage requires a new and deliberately balanced plan that details which goals to pursue and which activities and relationships to maintain. Achieving the defined goals while balancing the three spheres of influence (work, self, and home) are the keys to being happy during each lifestage.

Making a life plan is a lot like navigating a boat. You need to know about your vessel and the environment — how fast you're going, what direction you're headed, the speed and direction of the wind, the current status of the tide, the weather forecast. However, all of this navigational information is completely useless without one vital piece of information: your current position. You need to know where you are before you can set a course to a specific destination, which means you are truly lost if you're in the middle of the ocean with no visible landmarks. Life planning is exactly the same. If you don't know where you are, how can you realistically expect to define your future?

With knowledge about what happens in the various lifestages, you'll find it much easier to recognize where you are and what generally happens in your current lifestage. If you are in a transition period, this will also help you to bring some order out of the chaos that may surround you. In addition, familiarity with the lifestages will help you:

- Understand and accept yourself as you become more aware of your current lifestage and how it shapes your life.
- Point out your unique deviations from the norm.
- Find a new and productive balance between the three spheres of influence (work, self, home).
- Set priorities and make significant choices among your many options.
- Create a vision of your future and an awareness of what motivates you.
- Begin to think about the next lifestage you will enter and make appropriate plans.
- Establish and maintain a sense of direction that will enhance the quality of your life and bring you more control over your destiny.
- Help you to manage, work, and/or live with others who are perhaps on a different lifestage.

Your Vision of Success

Dream lofty dreams, and as you dream, so shall you become. Your vision is the promise of what you shall at last invent.
— John Ruskin[4]

"I believe this nation should commit itself to achieving the goal, before this decade is out, of landing a man on the moon and bringing him back safely to earth."[5] With those famous words, President John F. Kennedy proclaimed his vision to the nation — and gave it a deadline. This would prove to be a compelling and challenging dream for the United States that would ultimately lead to one of modern mankind's greatest achievements.

"I still have a dream. It is a dream deeply rooted in the American dream ... a dream that my four little children will one day live in a nation where they will not be judged by the color of their skin but by the content of their character."[6] Martin Luther King's "I Have a Dream" speech about racial equality and tolerance was an expression of a vision so powerful that it energized the nation around his nonviolent efforts to secure equal rights for black Americans.

Both John F. Kennedy and Martin Luther King, Jr., as visionary leaders, illustrate the incredible power that can come from a clear vision of how things can be. With an image of your desired future, that same power can be generated in your life. And nothing happens unless first you have a dream.

Look at your vision as a dream that you want to make real, as your ideal destination. If everything went the way you want, who would you be, where would you go, what would you do? Your vision statement is your lofty proclamation of your dreams for the future.

Before you attempt to create a vision for yourself, read through the following examples for each of the typical lifestages. These examples may help you express some of what you are feeling.

"My personal vision is to ..."

Youth (16–20)

... be the smartest, strongest, and best among my peers, and to have the ability to do whatever I set my mind to.

... test my physical and intellectual limits.

... achieve independence and gain the experience that will ensure that I achieve success in life.

Young Adult Transition (20–23)

... continue having fun and become all that I can be.

... have continuing, supportive relationships.

... figure out what to do with my life.

Emerging Career (23–28)

... excel in a world of opportunities where I can benefit from my education, be with my friends, enjoy life, and begin to settle down.

... develop my mind and improve my professional skills.

... be capable of dealing effectively and successfully with any challenges and opportunities I may encounter.

Settling Down Transition (28–30)

... find a way for the fun to continue.

... become all that I can be.

... figure out if there is more to life than work.

Settling Down & Grounding (30–40)

... be the best spouse/parent/friend and professional that I can be.

... make my mark in the world.

... reach a comfortable understanding and acceptance of my role in life.

... look at each new day as filled with opportunities that will propel me to prosperity.

Midlife Transition (40–45)

... derive satisfaction and a sense of accomplishment from my career.

... set goals that are realistic and that will lead to achievements.

... know what it will now take to be all that I can be.

... gain the strength of interdependence with my coworkers and my family.

Stability & Harvesting (45–60+)

... be mature, wise, happy, and content with my chosen life path.

... be at peace with my family, my community, and my work.

... be a mentor, to be someone others can look up to and enjoy working with.

... eventually stop working for money and settle into enjoying a long, fulfilling, and financially secure life surrounded by family and friends.

... fulfill my ongoing financial needs with part-time work that is intellectually stimulating.

Retirement Transition (60–65)

... use my new freedom to find out what else there is to life.

... explore fun activities and new opportunities now open to me.

... find ways I can continue to contribute my skills and talents to my family and community.

Post-Retirement (65+)

... be physically and mentally capable of staying in control of my affairs.

... continue to grow and explore life's possibilities.

... contribute to society, to be a friend and mentor to the young.

... be at peace with myself, to view each new day as a delightful gift while looking at my approaching death without fear.

When you are writing your vision statement, practice the art of expectancy. "In the long run men hit only what they aim at," Henry David Thoreau reminds us. "Therefore, though they should fail immediately, they had better aim at something high."[7] To which we might add, "Be careful what you aim for, you just might hit it!" Remember that in life you generally get what you expect. Positive thinking doesn't always work, but negative thinking always will!

Exercise
"My personal vision is ..."

Write down your own private dream, your personalized vision of the future. Since visualizing the rest of your life is difficult, consider where you would like to be at the end of your current lifestage. This is your vision, your dream for the future, so go ahead and think big! Your vision statement will not be a public document that you need to share with anyone, so let your true inner desires come out. You just may surprise yourself!

Begin your vision statement with "My personal vision is..." Review any notes you made while determining your own lifestage, and incorporate any thoughts you had about what you want to accomplish in this stage of your life. If you get stuck, refer back to the brief examples. Your goal is to create an inspiring vision statement that is anywhere from one sentence to one paragraph in length.

When you finish writing your vision statement, go through the quality checklist on page 46.

Quality Check

Your vision statement should evoke a clear image of your desire for the future. To ensure that this is true, check the following:

- Is your vision statement inspirational?
- Is it dynamic?
- Is it powerfully compelling?
- Is it challenging? (Stretch a bit!)
- Is it clear and easy to understand?
- Is it focused on the future?

Your Personal Motivators

Knowing others is wisdom, knowing yourself
is Enlightenment.
— Lao-tzu[8]

To find a way to live a balanced life in a tumultuous and rapidly changing world, you need to consciously be aware of what motivates you — physically, emotionally, and financially. Your personal motivators are the principles that guide your thoughts and actions. They are the essential elements of who you are. If you are constantly aware of your motivators, then you'll always have with you the drive to achieve your vision.

Some people call these "values," but we find that "motivators" is a more useful term that helps people to grasp the concept easily and apply it to their lives. These are the internal beliefs that motivate you to action. Think of your motivators as your helicopter's engine. They provide the power that drives your thoughts and actions. They guide your behavior toward achieving your vision and dictate your reactions to the challenges you face.

Your motivators represent what you will fight for. They represent your beliefs, your code of conduct, your accepted standard of behavior. Constant awareness of your personal motivators will stimulate you to action and help you avoid distractions. Motivators define meaning for the individual (and organizations, too). They are clear, uncompromising statements of what is critically important. Once found, they will help you define your purpose in life.

Your choice of motivators has been influenced by your parents, siblings, peers, and friends, by your education, upbringing, career choice, and work environment. Motivators vary from person to person, and they can change from one lifestage to another. Moreover, you can be influenced (or decide on your own) to change one or more of your motivators, thereby precipitating a dramatic change in your lifestyle or career.

Focusing on your motivators will spur your energy level. Knowing your motivators will help you avoid procrastination and achieve your vision of success. Identifying and remembering your personal motivators will help you develop (or confirm) a conscious life purpose.

Your motivators will guide your behavior as you move toward achievement of your vision. Conversely, if you move in a direction that is inconsistent with your motivators, you will probably fail. In fact, when things go wrong — at home or at work — it is usually because of a fundamental inconsistency between actions and motivators. Going against your nature is asking for failure.

Three Types of Motivators

Examples of the most common motivators are shown in Figure 2.2 on page 49. We have categorized these into three types: external motivators, internal motivators, and universal motivators.

External motivators are values typically imposed by others.

Internal motivators are basic values that underlie thought and motivate action.

Universal motivators are the characteristics that inspire excellence. They are guidelines for human conduct that have enduring value.

We have used the classification of motivators into these three categories because feedback from focus groups tells us that it is helpful to look at personal motivators within some sort of structure. How each individual perceives their own motivations will determine into which category any given motivator falls most appropriately. Some motivators may belong in all three categories. Sometimes an internal motivator for one person may actually be an external motivator for someone else.

Use the lists and the three-part division of motivators only as a jumping-off point. Embrace the motivators that may apply to you, and feel free to add motivators that you do not find here. The main thing to remember is that there is no "right" set of personal motivators. The core values that motivate you during any given lifestage are what make you unique. Your motivators will almost always be different from those selected by someone else.

Exercise
"I am motivated by . . . "

Using the list in Figure 2.2, check the motivators that you embrace most strongly and would fight for. Feel free to disregard those that don't apply to your lifestage, and add your own when necessary or appropriate. If you prefer, use a separate piece of paper to list your motivators.

Be honest with yourself. Select only those that you are passionate about. If you don't fully believe in your chosen motivators, then you will not go that extra mile for them. Since motivators help to define you, they must be freely chosen by you.

There is no "correct" number of motivators. Because we are all different, some people may only need a few motivators to define themselves (navigate their own helicopter), while others may need close to a dozen. To ensure that they are truly core motivators, do not select more than ten or twelve. Then go to the quality check on page 50.

External Motivators

Acceptance
Balanced budgeting
Community
Competition
Consensus
Customer satisfaction
Deadlines
Discipline
Empowerment
Environmental care
Fame
Family harmony
Friendships
Growth of business
Health and fitness
Honorable behavior
Justice
Love
Physical image
Physical security
Prestige
Relationships
Respect
Stability
Status, recognition
Team spirit
Tolerance
Tradition

Internal Motivators

Accuracy
Achievement
Balance in life
Career success
Caring for someone
Challenge

Common sense
Competence
Control
Diligence
Discipline
Diversity
Fairness
Financial security
Freedom
Fun
Happiness
High energy level
Independence
Intellectual growth
Knowledge
Learning
Lifestyle
Life fulfillment
Material possessions
Money
Personal appearance
Personal skills to develop:
    Artistic
    Communication
    Crisis management
    Decision making
    Diplomacy
    Knowledge
    Language
    Leadership
    Manual
    Problem solving
    Technical
    Writing skills
Prudence
Power
Security

Spiritual growth
Trusting others
Truth
Winning
Work

Universal Motivators

Caring
Civic virtue
Courage
Creativity
Determination
Effort
Encouragement
Enthusiasm
Ethics
Excellence
Excitement
Expectancy
Generosity
Growth
Honesty
Human dignity
Humility
Imagination
Inspiration
Integrity
Loyalty
Patience
Perseverance
Persistence
Quality
Resourcefulness
Responsibility
Service
Sincerity
Trustworthiness

Figure 2.2
Common motivators

Quality Check

Your motivators should represent the values that drive your life. To ensure that this is true, check the following:

- Are the motivators you have selected the core values driving your life?
- Will your chosen motivators empower you toward achievement of your vision?
- Are you willing to fight for each motivator on your list?
- Taken as a group, do they accurately describe you?

Your Purpose in Life

The great and glorious masterpiece of man is how to live with a purpose.
— Michel de Montaigne[9]

With your vision statement and your motivators firmly in mind, you can now proceed to write out what you consider to be your purpose in life — your mission, your reason for being alive. Think of your purpose as the direction you will take to achieve your vision while being guided by your motivators.

Your purpose should redefine your lofty vision into a specific direction. This is where the tires hit the road on your journey through life. Your purpose is your passion, what gives your life meaning, your reason for doing what you do each day.

Your statement of purpose should be a simple, positive statement of why you are here. Like the needle of a compass, you'll use it to find a direction through life and validate your progress. A purpose is not a goal that can be reached, but rather a direction like "west." No matter how far west you go, you can still go farther west. Just as a compass guides a sailor, your purpose will become a consistent guide to help you set your course. Whenever you are "on course," you are "on purpose" — that is a powerful and wonderful feeling to have.

Everything becomes easy, effortless, and enjoyable if you are clear about your purpose in life, if you can relate every daily decision and activity to your purpose. Together with your vision and your motivators, your purpose continues to answer the question of why you are on this journey we call life.

Your purpose will also help you identify appropriate steps to take whenever you find yourself in turmoil and uncertain of what to do next. The act of writing down your purpose will reinforce it, help you to remember it, and set you on the direct path to making it a reality. You'll find your purpose will help you stay in control.

Establishing a purpose will reduce stress and promote effectiveness in your life. Your purpose will strengthen your feelings of self-worth, help you stay focused on positive outcomes, and guide you as you improve the balance between your personal and your professional life.

In fact, having a written purpose and referring to it frequently is so vital to success that we recommend you carry it with you. Some of our clients think it is so important that they post it on their bathroom mirror so it is the first thing they see each morning and the last thing they see each night before going to bed.

To give you a better feel for purpose statements, we have compiled some examples for three different lifestages. Please keep in mind that purpose statements are the most important and personal definition of yourself that you can create. As such, we put forth these examples with some reservation. Read them only as examples. Do not let them influence your thoughts or steer you in a direction that is not clearly yours.

"My purpose in life is to ..."

Emerging Career (23–28)

- Use all my technical skills and persuasive powers to protect and preserve the environment, and simultaneously to demonstrate that a single mother can have a professional career and raise happy, well-balanced kids. (Motivators: environmental care, engineering skills, enthusiasm, family harmony, challenge, caring.)

- Build homes that are ecologically and technically of the highest quality, yet beautiful and affordable to the middle class; to succeed in the construction industry while being a devoted father and lay preacher. (Motivators: community, spiritual growth, creativity, manual skills, customer satisfaction, financial success, trustworthiness.)

Stability & Harvesting (45–60+)

- Introduce to people the planning tools and techniques that promote purposeful, productive, and happy lives with a healthy balance between the needs of work, family, and self. (Motivators: balance in life, problem-solving skills, integrity, creativity, life fulfillment, fun.)

- Use my knowledge of philosophy and clinical psychology to help people grow and experience peace of mind; to demonstrate that a woman can single-handedly race a catamaran on the same competitive level as men. (Motivators: intellectual growth, spiritual growth, caring, physical daring, recognition, competition.)

Retirement Transition (60–65)

- Use my interest in archaeology, my technical skills in the field of marine engineering, and my business experience to recover historical artifacts from sunken vessels in the Caribbean. (Motivators: engineering skills, achievement, tradition, expectancy, fun, material possessions, perseverance.)

- Perform as a pianist with the local chamber music ensemble, and to teach music appreciation to children. (Motivators: piano skills, music appreciation, determination, discipline, inspiration, status, recognition, life fulfillment.)

The Career Dilemma

The reality of our world is that only a very small number of people find their purpose in their current work. Most people look at their work as a paycheck rather than as a fulfillment of their purpose in life, but there are exceptions. Many teachers continue to work under less than ideal conditions because they love teaching children. Most clergy are not paid to run a business, but they do similar administrative work because they are committed to serving their congregation. Many family physicians choose not to specialize so they can maintain ongoing relationships with their patients and have more time for their family.

With a huge leap of faith and no small amount of effort, it is possible to achieve your purpose while working. It is not uncommon to hear of someone radically shifting their career, say from being an attorney to becoming a counselor for inner-city youth. This is undoubtedly someone with the intelligence to define a life purpose, but also the courage and conviction to truly follow it.

These people are inspired by their work. They are profoundly interested in what they do for a living, persist in it, and eventually excel in their chosen profession, even though few stay with their initial line of work.

Frequently, those who don't find success and happiness in their careers reverse this process. Their only objective is to make enough money to *someday* quit their jobs and then do what they "really" wanted to do. They typically seek get-rich-quick schemes while continuing to work at unfulfilling jobs.

Clearly, if you do what you love first, success and happiness will follow. We call this "living on purpose."

Risking It All*

Brian Hieggelke: Money Can't Buy Me Love

Brian Hieggelke had the life most people dream of: In his 20s he was raking in $200,000 a year as an investment broker for Goldman Sachs & Co. What's more, the young MBA had an expense account, full health benefits, and the potential to double his income within a few years. A rising star at the company, his career path up the corporate ladder seemed inevitable.

For the first few years, Hieggelke reveled in the hurly-burly of the stock market — including the crash in 1987. But as his tenure at the company grew, his enthusiasm diminished. Hawking investments to multimillionaires from a big office overlooking the Windy City lost its luster. Once he'd mastered the art of selling, his dream job became routine, uncreative. There were few skills left for him to master. He needed a change — and he was willing to risk it all for self-employment.

After re-evaluating his priorities, Hieggelke discovered that "money alone wasn't going to do it." He wanted more creativity in his life, so he began searching for an escape route. One night in 1985, while sitting around the kitchen table with his wife and younger brother, he hit on an idea that would alter the course of his career: starting a local paper for his gentrified Chicago neighborhood. Despite hefty credit card balances and two student loans, Hieggelke put his assets on the line and initially invested $20,000 to launch *NewCity*, a local weekly newspaper.

Don't be fooled, however: Pursuing your dream — no matter how much you were previously making — takes perseverance. For two years, Hieggelke struggled to turn his vision into reality. He put in grueling 12-hour days at Goldman's and then raced to the paper where he crunched numbers, read manuscripts, and approved layouts until midnight. "It was a hectic time," he recalls." And although most of his spare time was being pumped into the paper, *NewCity* was still losing money

---

— "because I wasn't able to devote my full attention to making the paper work," he says.

With his sights set on turning his dream into a profitable venture, Hieggelke marched into his boss's office one morning with his resignation in hand. At a time when most of corporate America was downsizing and unemployment lines were littered with out-of-work executives, Hieggelke was sacrificing his security — and there was nothing anyone could do to persuade him to stay. "Everyone thought I was crazy," he recalls.

Once taking over the helm, the pressure was on him to pull the paper into the black. What's more, his wife announced she was pregnant. With hospital bills mounting, another mouth to feed, and no $200,000 paycheck to cover expenses, Hieggelke was forced to change his high-flying lifestyle. For the next year, his family of five survived on his diminishing savings and credit card loans — all without taking a dime out of the company.

"I was an impetuous youth who thought I was going to be making so much money that I wasn't going to have to worry. I just didn't realize how long it was going to take to build," he says. Despite poor financial forecasting, Hieggelke insists he never suffered sleepless nights: "I've got a ludicrous threshold for risk."

Now at 33, Hieggelke still thrives on risk and has few regrets about leaving his job. *NewCity* offers him the opportunity to sell his own vision — instead of someone else's. And the paper boasts annual revenues of more than $1 million, has a circulation of 64,000, and employs 23 people.

Jill Gabbe: Shifting Personal Priorities

For years, Jill Gabbe's husband had been hounding her to take the plunge — leave her corporate job and join forces with him in his marketing company. But working as a public relations exec at a Manhattan identity and image management consulting firm had pluses she just

Continued on page 56

Risking It All

Continued from page 55

couldn't resist: a seat on the board, a three-person staff, full health coverage, several stock incentive plans, and a salary of $130,000 a year plus bonuses.

But as her years in the executive suite grew, Gabbe found fewer opportunities to exercise new skills. Like Hieggelke, she felt an unshakable need to make a career change. To top it off, her personal priorities were shifting. "I had two children, and I wanted a more flexible work schedule," she says.

In a corporate environment, everyone's treated equally. You're required to put in X amount of hours — no matter how productive you are — and your superiors want to know where you are all the time. The motivation to do better is stifled. For Gabbe, an inflexible work schedule began to take its toll.

Recognizing her malaise, Gabbe's husband sat down with her and suggested she either take a leave of absence to analyze her career — or reconsider working with him. This time, his request didn't fall on deaf ears. After months of job hunting, she mentally ran through a list of companies that, instead of hiring her as an employee, could become the first clients in her own firm. Two months later, she joined her husband in Gabbe & Gabbe, their new public relations and multimedia marketing firm.

This executive turned entrepreneur has no regrets about leaving her six-figure salary. The freedom and flexibility she's gained allow her to set her own business hours and get more involved with her kids. Psychologically, she says she feels more secure today. "In a corporation the idea that you have a job for life is gone," she says. "But if you go out and do it on your own, then you control your own destiny." What's more, her earning potential is now unlimited: Gabbe & Gabbe bills about $1.5 million annually.

Exercise
"My purpose in life is ..."

Reread your vision statement and your list of motivators, then in your mind think about how you answer the question "What is my purpose in life?" This exercise will be especially challenging if you look at your current job as merely a way to earn money. You need to answer the additional question "Is there something else I'd rather be doing?"

Some people find it helpful to think about a time when life (including work) seemed effortless: a time when you were having fun and enjoying every aspect of life, a point in your life when time seemed to pass quickly and your body never fatigued. Examining the causes of this bliss will help you determine what you really love to do and live for. This should become the central component of your purpose. When you finish writing your purpose, go to the quality check below.

Quality Check

Your statement of purpose should clearly define the reasons for your daily actions. To ensure that this is true, check the following:

- Is your purpose statement a true reflection of what is motivating you toward your vision?
- Will it truly inspire you to achieve your vision?
- Is it something you would be proud to post on your bathroom mirror?
- Is it something you would enjoy doing?

And don't forget — *work should be fun.* If you are spending forty or more hours a week at something that isn't fun, you need to study your vision and your motivators, then find something else to do with your life (i.e., develop a new purpose). It might help to look at the career dilemma from another angle: Every hour wasted at unfulfilling work is an hour you could have enjoyed at home with your family or friends.

"Having fun" is one of the core work motivators we use to evaluate everything we do in our business. Quite simply, if it's not fun, we don't do it. Consistent use of this motivator as a decision criteria has undoubtedly cost us some business, but it has also allowed us to avoid burnout and lead highly satisfying lives. As a result of this commitment to having fun, we have dramatically increased the number of successful products and initiatives in our business. A high level of enthusiasm and energy is the guarantee of our success.

What is success? Much like happiness, success means something different to each of us. Rather than being measured in dollars, success for most of us is about happiness and the ability to enjoy a balanced life. It is about achieving the goals that give you satisfaction and allow you to feel fulfilled and worthwhile.

Looking Ahead

Once you have defined your vision, your motivators, and your purpose, you have built a very solid foundation for creating a meaningful plan for the next segment of your life. This foundation is a central component to achieving a balanced and successful life. The next step, creating a detailed plan for achieving your vision of success, is covered in Chapter 3.

C H A P T E R   3

The Planning Mode

A life that hasn't a definite plan is likely to become driftwood.

— David Sarnoff[1]

YOU HAVE NOW COME TO THE PLANNING phase as you continue to prepare for your journey through life. In Chapter 2 you pinpointed your current lifestage and built the foundation of your plan with an examination of your vision, your motivators, and your life purpose. You are now ready to create a dynamic and balanced plan for your future.

You cannot expect to go through life without a plan and end up with anything but random happenings and uncertain (and perhaps undesirable) outcomes. Planning for the rest of your life is next to impossible, but planning for your current or next lifestage is not. If you want to be successful and happy, you need to develop a balanced lifestage plan, and you need to make sure your plan is aligned with your vision, your motivators, and your purpose. If you leave success up to chance, you will undoubtedly lose out on your full potential.

Before you begin thinking about your future, you must let go of the past, especially anything unresolved that may be having an adverse effect on you in the present. The simplest way to do this is to realize that none of us can change yesterday, but everyone can change tomorrow. You can learn from mistakes you've made and then move on, hopefully avoiding the same pitfalls.[2]

Begin with an Overview

He who determines the end, provides the means.
— Benedetto Varchi, *L'Ercolano*[3]

Now you're ready to start making plans, one lifestage at a time. Look at the sampling of plans that follows, paying particular attention to the lifestage where you are and the lifestage that is coming up next.

Exercise
Make a Preliminary Plan

Take a helicopter overview of your life by scanning the sampling of lifestage plans shown on the following pages. As you read the examples, check those items (or list them on a separate sheet of paper) that seem to express your current situation. Remember that the plans given here are merely suggestions designed to stimulate your thinking process. Make notes pertaining to your own life: past, present, and future. Write down any preliminary lifestage planning ideas you have.

"During this stage of my life, I want to ..."

Youth (16–20)

- Find a part-time job and save half of my income for my future education.
- Begin thinking about various professions and careers that interest me.

- Concentrate on getting a good education.
- Learn good study habits.
- Develop the habit of regular exercise.
- Learn to speed-read.
- Learn to play a musical instrument or find some other hobby.

Family & Lifestyle
- Participate in team sports.
- Become a mentor for my siblings.

Personal Finances
- Learn to live within my monthly budget.

Friends & Community
- Join a youth group.
- Participate in competitive sports.

Young Adult Transition (20–23)

- Investigate various career paths.
- Look for a role model to emulate.

- See more of the world before I make work and family commitments.
- Spend a semester studying abroad.
- Create a balanced lifestage plan for my remaining college years.
- Begin the habit of taking a weekly overview of my life.

Family & Lifestyle

- Experience living away from my parents.
- Begin to create a more adult relationship with my parents.

Personal Finances

- Budget for a year or more at a time.
- Force myself to live within the budget I set.

Friends & Community

- Reevaluate my relationships to make sure they are meaningful.
- Join a fraternity/sorority.

Emerging Career (23–28)

- Select a career I will enjoy, one that utilizes my strengths and that is in alignment with my motivators.
- Hunt for a challenging, well-paid job with opportunities for career advancement.
- Explore alternate career paths and work opportunities.
- Don't be afraid to make mistakes. I'll learn and grow from them.
- Develop the habit of celebrating my victories.

- Set up a fitness program that will keep me healthy and in good shape into my midlife years.
- Consider getting a graduate degree.
- Figure out if getting a professional license will be advantageous to me and, if so, begin the required process.
- Create a new, balanced lifestage plan; include all the areas of responsibility that pertain to my full-time job.
- Make sure that my lifestage plan will stretch and challenge me without defeating me.
- Make no small plans, but remember to smell the flowers along the way.

Family & Lifestyle

- Set up my own household.
- Consider getting married and starting a family.

Personal Finances

- Develop a budget that pays off my debts, gives me financial independence, and allows for some savings.
- Consider working overtime to pay off educational loans and gain independence.
- Begin saving for the purchase of a home.
- Begin an incremental investment program, building in some liquidity and a relatively high-risk tolerance for a potentially higher return.
- Write a will as soon as I get married or have a child.
- Buy an adequate amount of life insurance to cover my family.

Friends & Community

- Test and solidify my relationships.
- Consider volunteering to work for a cause I believe in.
- Maintain contact with old friends as they move about.

Settling Down Transition (28–30)

- Reassess my future career objectives.
- Employ my youthful strengths to take courageous leaps after weighing the pros and cons. Fortune favors the bold.

- Try to define what happiness means to me and what my purpose in life should be.
- Update my lifestage plan in a manner that will make the next stage of my life both meaningful and enjoyable.
- Take some calculated risks.
- Consider going back to school for career advancement.

Family & Lifestyle

- Change or confirm my selection of lifestyle.
- Each week set aside some quality time to spend with my spouse and children.
- Make sure that my plan for the next stage of my life is in harmony with the plan of my spouse.

Personal Finances

- Critique my financial performance since college.
- Decide on a savings and investment program for the next ten years.

Friends & Community

- Change or confirm my selection of community.
- Seek out ways to avoid feeling lonely.
- Decide which friends are likely to remain important to me and renew my efforts to stay in contact with them.

Settling Down & Grounding (30–40)

- Work for professional recognition.
- Look for a mentor in my profession — where I work, in my community, or at the local university.
- Explore alternate, fulfilling career options.
- In my role of senior manager, make a business strategic plan to match my ambitions.
- Take calculated risks to further my career success.
- Celebrate victories with my team.

- Write down my vision of where I'd like to be in one, five, and ten years. Free myself from the limitations of my past and dream big.
- Plan my action steps to fit my vision for the future.
- Regularly refer to my vision for inspiration.
- Maintain a fitness program that will enable me to stay healthy and in good shape.

- Involve myself in new leisure activities.
- Reflect on all of the key areas of my life on a weekly basis.

Family & Lifestyle

- Solidify my marriage and my relationship with my children.
- Take time out to enjoy living.
- Each week set aside quality time to spend with my spouse and children.
- Plan and enjoy family vacations.
- Periodically check children's development against my own value system.
- Plan the best possible education for my children.

Personal Finances

- Make a personal and family budget that maximizes my contribution to a retirement fund.
- Aggressively invest my long-term savings for maximum ultimate return.
- Work with an attorney to draw up a will, a living will, and a power of attorney for myself and my spouse.

Friends & Community

- Join a service club and/or a professional organization that makes contribututions to my community.
- Join a community group for increased companionship.

Midlife Transition (40–45)

- Evaluate my career to ensure it will continue to be satisfying and give me a sense of accomplishment. Consider if perhaps I should change career path or direction.
- Assess the gap between my achievements and my aspirations, then set more realistic goals for the future.
- Look for something new and interesting to be excited about.

- Being true to myself, decide what my purpose in this lifestage should be.
- Establish clear, positive expectations about life and about how I'll continue to grow and develop.
- Recognize that it is still not too late to take some calculated risks.
- Decide what I would most like to contribute in the next stage of my life.
- Create a new, balanced lifestage plan to support my decisions.
- Keep remembering that without a written plan my dreams will not come true.

Family & Lifestyle
- Confirm (or change) my selection of lifestyle and community.
- Decide which material possessions I really want and which I can do without.
- Make sure that my plan for the next stage of my life is acceptable to and in harmony with my spouse's plan.

Personal Finances
- Evaluate which kind of luxuries I can afford and which I cannot.
- Start (or continue) a serious retirement savings plan.

Friends & Community
- Seek out ways to avoid feeling lonely.
- Join (or continue to be active in) affinity groups or organizations.

Stability & Harvesting (45–60+)

- Redefine what success means to me.
- In my role as a senior manager, make a business strategic plan to match my lifestage plan.

- Solidify my position for happiness, security, and income maximization.
- Begin looking for and grooming a successor.
- Find people for whom I can be a mentor.
- Remember that I will reach my highest goals only with the help of other people. Celebrate my victories with them.

- Enjoy life while I am at my peak.
- Remember that if I refuse to accept anything but the best, then I have a better chance of getting the best.
- Intensify my involvement in leisure activities, including those that will help me stay in shape into old age.
- Read up on retirement options and begin retirement planning in earnest.
- Check out the American Association of Retired People (AARP) to learn about the many benefits and options available to me.
- Learn the skills I'll need to keep myself occupied in retirement, whether through part-time work or as a volunteer.
- Continue the habit of a weekly overview session of my life.

Family & Lifestyle

- Seek mature love and intimacy.
- Establish a comfortable home and lifestyle.
- Mentor and support my children through college.
- Explore the world while I am still relatively young and can afford to travel.
- Plan vacations to look into alternative locations where I can live in retirement.
- Study lifestyles of people in retirement to determine what will be most suitable for me.
- Consider the pros and cons of purchasing my retirement home in advance.

- Arrange care for my elderly parent(s).
- Begin to sell or give away personal possessions to simplify life in retirement.

Personal Finances

- Evaluate my need (taking inflation into account) for continuing to work for money in retirement and/or my willingness to live on less.
- Maximize the input into my retirement plan.
- Diversify my retirement funds for security and growth.
- Verify my anticipated Social Security income.
- Determine when I can afford to retire, then set a tentative date.
- Try living for several months on my anticipated retirement income to determine how well my financial plans fit my desired lifestyle.

Friends & Community

- Experiment with volunteer activities that I might enjoy now and in retirement.
- Nurture and protect my long-term friendships.
- Seek new friends by joining clubs centered on my hobbies and interests.

Retirement Transition (60–65)

- Begin to take time off from work to create room for other things in my life.
- Look for an interesting part-time job, volunteer position, or board membership.

- Renew my vision for the future and make sure it includes a positive expectation about and anticipation of the rest of my life.
- Create a new, balanced lifestage plan for my later years, based upon a blend of pleasure activities and some sort of

mission that will allow me to retain the feeling that my life has a genuine purpose.

- Allow lots of time for spontaneous detours.

Family & Lifestyle

- Consider taking a special vacation to launch my retirement.
- Settle into my retirement home and/or community.
- Make sure that my own plan for the next stage of my life is in harmony with my spouse's plan.
- Arrange for simplicity and functional comfort at home.

Personal Finances

- Determine the amount of my pension benefits and decide if I want to receive a lump sum for investment or annuity purposes.
- Taking inflation into account, prepare personal cash flow projections for the next ten, twenty, and thirty years.
- Make alternative projections in case I (or my spouse) am left alone.
- Decide when and how to begin collecting Social Security benefits for myself and my spouse.
- Make an estate plan to minimize taxes; share the details with my spouse and/or children.

Friends & Community

- Join community organizations for companionship and a sense of belonging.
- Look for new friends.

Post-Retirement (65+)

- Look for (or continue) a mentoring role.
- Look for consulting roles where I can share my wisdom and professional experience, without having day to day responsibilities.

- Plan the life I feel I deserve — free of constraints and with a significant amount of fun.
- Refocus my priorities to fit my energy level and style.
- Consider seeing more of the world.
- Explore the meaning of life by studying philosophy, history, and religion.
- Make an effort to continue to understand the world around me.
- Resist the temptation to stop growing and contributing.
- Explore my roots.
- Try new hobbies and develop new skills. Continue learning.
- Work at maintaining my health, retaining my skills, and keeping a positive attitude.
- Focus on my spiritual growth, and continue to seek wisdom and inner harmony.

 Family & Lifestyle

- Seek opportunities for fun family gatherings.
- Plan more family and group travel.
- Look after my home without overdoing it.
- Show interest in my children and grandchildren.
- Look for opportunities to share my wisdom and life experience.

Personal Finances

- Arrange for supplemental Medicare insurance.
- Decide on a spending strategy in five- and ten-year increments to maximize my happiness, independence, and security, and with spending gradually diminishing in step with my energy level.
- Gradually give away excess assets to family, friends, or charity.

Friends & Community

- Continue to look for new friends and new experiences to share with them.
- Look for new experiences as well as new opportunities to make the world a better place to live.
- Find opportunities for volunteering and otherwise giving something back to my community.

Define Your Key Result Areas

Key result areas are the main areas of performance and responsibility on which you must concentrate your efforts and resources in order to achieve your unique job-related and personal vision of success.

— Kim Norup and Willy Norup[4]

As you have seen throughout this book, the three spheres of influence (work, self, and home) provide a useful model for examining life and evaluating its balance. Now let's look at a complementary concept that will help you apply the spheres of influence to specific and logical segments of your life, in particular those that are most important to you.

This concept, based on an ancient Oriental technique for memorization and memory enhancement, is called key result areas. It allows you to keep many items in your mind by imagining them as being filed into separate and clearly labeled compartments from which they can be retrieved when needed. Years ago the discovery of this memorization technique led us to draw a parallel to the concept of key result areas (first mentioned by the noted business professor and author, Peter Drucker).[5] We realized that having a physical tool to allow for the arrangement of one's life within a set of life-encompassing key result areas would be a powerful extension of the "mental compartments" technique.

For our purposes, then, *key result areas are the main areas of performance and responsibility on which you must concentrate your efforts and resources in order to achieve your unique vision of the future.* Your key result areas are the results-producing elements of your life, and as a group they should completely cover your three spheres of influence (work, self, and home).

Using your own personally defined key result areas, you will be able to plan your lifestages by gathering together your dreams and setting your goals in an organized fashion. Having organized your life into these separate segments, you can much more easily manage and control your future. You can approach the opportunities and meet the challenges in your life one at a time, while you systematically plan, monitor, and record what you do.

This simple technique of setting up a personal set of key result areas will empower you to maintain balance in your life while avoiding chaos, confusion, and overload. You will have an increased sense of being in control and a reduced sense of uncertainty. Making decisions will become easier. The details kept within your key result areas will help you decide which activities will lead you directly to your vision of success. Whenever you scan your key result area files, you will also have instantaneous access to that helicopter overview so necessary for staying in control and meeting your objectives.

Universal Key Result Areas

Certain key result areas are common to almost everyone, while others are specific to the way various individuals live and work. Based upon our extensive experience and research through a broad cross-section of industries and professions, we have found the following set of key result areas to have an almost universal application. As you read through them, decide for yourself which would work for you.

- Life overview

- Workplace overview
- Financial data & control
- Productivity & quality
- Human resources
- Customer relations

- Self-development
- Health & fitness

- Personal finances
- Family & lifestyle
- Friends & community

This universal set of common key result areas can be used as the jumping off point for your own personal lifestage plan. This doesn't mean that you must use these particular key result areas or name them exactly the way we did. Customize the list to fit your unique work and personal requirements.

Customized Key Result Areas

Each of us is unique. Not only are we at different lifestages, but we also take different paths on our journey through life. Because we are complex people with different needs, desires, fears, responsibilities, and roles, we each have our own priorities in life. Consequently, we will have different interpretations of the key result areas that uniquely describe us.

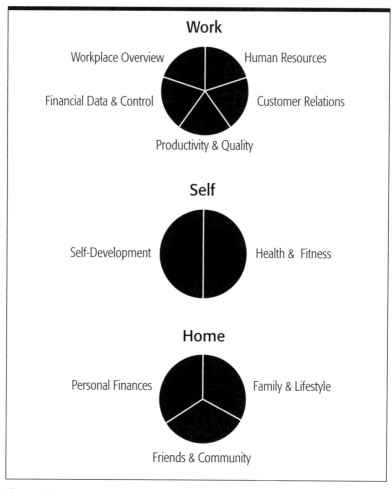

Figure 3.1
Three spheres of influence divided into key result areas

Customizing the list of common key result areas presented here will allow you to create a powerful life management system that gives attention to all the important aspects of your life. The personal key result areas you select should cover all the important aspects in each of the three spheres of influence: your work, your self, and your home (including family, friends, and community). Whether you're a CEO, an artist, a homemaker, or a student, your set of key result areas will be uniquely yours. They will not be exactly the same for any two people, yet they may share common elements — a hobby, a fitness activity, family commitments, work, religion.

As an example, the key result areas used by Willy and Kim are shown here. Willy is currently in the retirement transition stage of his life, while Kim is in the settling down and grounding stage. The key result areas illustrate how the duties of their business are split and how the remainder of their time is used for their individual talents and interests.

Willy's Key Result Areas

- Life overview

- Geodex overview
- Management succession
- Corporate finances
- Books & newsletters
- Consultants
- Research & development

- Painting
- Sailing

- Personal finances
- Investments
- Tax & legal matters
- Home & cabin
- Family
- Travel

Kim's Key Result Areas

- Life overview

- Geodex overview
- Financial data & control
- Team & teamwork
- Quality, productivity, service
- Marketing
- Direct sales
- Inventory & overhead control
- Plant & equipment
- Books & newsletters

- Self-development
- Golf & fitness

- Family & lifestyle
- House & garden
- Personal finances

Exercise
List Your Key Result Areas

Create a list of your key result areas by dividing each of your spheres of influence (work, self, and home) into clearly defined segments. As you work on your list of key result areas, follow these suggestions:

- Every item on your list should have measurable results.
- Do not set up key result areas for activities and daily routine tasks that are not in themselves leading to important and measurable results. ("Meetings" is a good example of this kind of activity.)
- Make the name for each key result area clear and unambiguous by using no more than three words.
- Be sure all of your interests and responsibilities in life are covered.
- As a group, your key result areas should represent all of your output, interests, and responsibilities — with minimal overlaps from one key result area to another.

For a detailed listing of profession-specific examples, see the job-related key result areas tabulated in Appendix 1. The lists there will give you more ideas on how to establish the best combination that together will cover all of your results-oriented work responsibilities.

Managing your life in logical key result areas will provide a flexible framework in which to dream, plan, and work toward your vision of the future, while being true to your vision, motivators, and purpose in life. When you have given careful consideration to the selection of your own personal set of key result areas, the planning process easily follows.

Define Your Objectives

> *Our plans miscarry because they have no aim. When a man does not know what harbor he is making for, no wind is the right wind.*
>
> — Seneca (4 B.C.–A.D. 65)[6]

To get where you want to go, you must set specific goals for each of your key result areas. We call these "objectives." With your objectives clearly defined and readily accessible, you'll never be at a loss as to which direction to go.

Objectives are statements of intent, and they describe results that will be achieved within specific time frames. Objectives can and should be developed into detailed, step-by-step action plans. In this way, you break your vision down into specific steps that will become the driving force behind your day-to-day actions.

Objectives must be in written form. An objective in your head is merely wishful thinking. An objective on paper is the first and most important step required to assure significant results. Well-written objectives not only specify the action to be taken, but also stimulate that action. Taking the time to write your objectives pays off dramatically in results! They will become the driving force behind your day-to-day work and life. Study these examples before you write your own objectives.

"My objective is to…"

Life Overview

- Finish my lifestage plan within a week and then immediately schedule its implementation.

Workplace Overview

- Develop and adopt a new mission statement for the organization, and distribute it to all personnel by July 31.
- Translate the organization's mission into fiscal year objectives for all five departments by September 15.

Financial Data & Control
- Install zero-based budgeting in all departments by September 15.
- During the fourth quarter, implement a minimum of four ways to avoid budget overruns.

Productivity & Quality
- Reduce number of service complaints by 50 percent before October 30.

Human Resources
- Complete management succession and development plan for top three levels by February 14, at time expenditure of 200 hours max.

Customer Relations
- At a cost of $8,500 and before end of third quarter, conduct phone survey of external customers to determine specific needs and areas of service improvement.
- Work with each department to determine whether it meets or exceeds the needs and expectations of all its internal customers, and ask each department head to write a summary report with suggested improvement plans that is due to me no later than June 15.

 Self-Development
- Before May 12, implement the ideas that I have noted from the book *Life Beyond Time Management.*
- Before April 15, complete my career plan for the next five years, and schedule time during the next twelve months to assure its success.

Health & Fitness
- Three times a week block off one hour for exercise that will make me work up a sweat.

 Personal Finances
- By the end of December, project financial needs for a new home, and set up a savings and investment plan to match.

Family & Lifestyle

- By August 15, remodel the attic at a cost of $5,000 max.
- Guide and help my daughter with her college applications, and make sure they are mailed no later than February 1.

Friends & Community

- By the end of December, collect $3,000 toward the new church spire fund.

Exercise
Write Your Objectives

For each of the key result areas you have on your customized list, write an objective that includes the following three parts:

WHAT. Your objectives must be realistic, specific, and confined to a single theme.

HOW MUCH (or HOW WELL or HOW MANY). Your objectives must be measurable.

BY WHEN. Your objectives must include realistic target dates or deadlines.

Another useful guideline for writing complete, meaningful, and useful objectives is to make them SMARTER:

Specific: Be very clear about the outcome you desire.

Measurable: Quantify your objective so you can measure progress and completion.

Achievable: Your objective must be in the realm of the possible.

Results-oriented: Your objective must lead to an outcome that can be realized by the taking of specific actions.

Time-bounded: Set a duration and a deadline for your activity.

Exciting: To be effective (and to ensure completion), your objective must excite you, and it must not conflict with your vision, your motivators, and your purpose in life.

Readily available: Keep your objectives and action plans out in a place where they are easily assessible.

Make a Results-Oriented Lifestage Plan

Make the most of today. Translate your good intentions into actual deeds. Know that you can do what ought to be done. Improve your plans. Keep a definite goal of achievement constantly in view. Realize that work well and worthily done makes life truly worth living.

— Grenville Kleiser[7]

Over the years we have been in contact with many high-achievers. These are executives, professionals, managers, military officers, entrepreneurs, homemakers and students who share one common characteristic: The status quo is just not good enough. These people clearly want more out of life.

High-achievers come to us in search of effective tools and techniques to help them achieve even more, but many of them exhibit the same disturbing characteristic. They have not put sufficient thought into the future they desire, nor have they given any consideration to what really makes them feel happy and fulfilled. Many of them spend much more time planning their next vacation than they have ever spent planning the next stage of their life! Tragic, but true.

We frequently receive fan mail from clients who describe for us how the planning tools we developed have helped them achieve some truly incredible results. While these letters warm our hearts and give great meaning to our daily tasks, not many of them can top the feedback Kim recently received at a meeting of advisors who work with the local school district on various business-related issues. The topic of conversation was how to help every freshman at the local high school develop a personal five-year plan.

At the conclusion of the meeting, a young woman recounted her experience with life planning. Due to a very traumatic and abusive home life, she realized as a high school student that she would have to be self-sufficient immediately after graduation. Through pure coincidence she happened to come upon a planning system that she credits with giving her the ability to achieve the success she was currently enjoying in the business world. She told the story to the entire group, not realizing that Kim's company had developed the planning system that turned her life around.

This young woman was highly motivated even as a teenager, but the vast majority of people become adults (whether that is defined as graduating from college, entering the workforce, or getting married and starting a family) without the slightest idea of what makes them happy, let alone what they want to achieve in life. They hit the ground running and don't look back. Only many years later, perhaps when they find themselves in midlife crisis, do they stop to think about these vital issues.

No matter which lifestage you find yourself in, by doing this important thinking now, you will have a huge head start in creating greater meaning and happiness in your life. It's never too late to plan for success. Developing your lifestage plan will allow you to be a leader of your life, to be a pilot instead of a passenger on your journey. Your lifestage plan will help you define where you want to go and then create the specific action plans necessary for getting there. Personal success, then, becomes the ability to effectively manage your life from vision to results.

You've already written meaningful objectives for each of your key result areas. In your plan, you will need to prioritize these objectives and align them to avoid conflicts, all with the goal of maintaining balance between your three spheres of influence. Instead of attempting to do many things at the same time, you must decide which are the most important to you, your work, and your family now. With their estimated completion dates in mind, you can begin to plan for the logical time when the next set of objectives should receive your attention.

When you're finished, you will have established where you are, where you would like to go, what you must do to get there within a given time frame. As your lifestage plan takes shape, it becomes a map you can use as you navigate through life.

Writing a balanced lifestage plan will take some effort, but the results will be well worth the time spent. The information presented here will help you in an effective and straight-forward way.

As you work on your lifestage plan, remember that you are a unique individual and your plan should reflect this. How you plan

Exercise
Use Your Intuition

As you plan, don't be afraid to follow your intuition and go with what immediately feels right to you. More often than not, this turns out for the best! When in doubt, try this powerful three-step process for intuitively making effective decisions:

Step 1
Sit comfortably, close your eyes, and spend a few minutes trying to completely relax your mind and your body.

Step 2
Slowly open your eyes, and focus on the decision to be made.

Step 3
Tell yourself, "Now it's decision time," and then decide to do the first thing that comes to your mind! This will be your gut reaction, drawing on everything you have learned so far in life, and you can do a lot worse than following that.

your life will differ from how others plan their lives. If you have family obligations (a career-seeking spouse, aging parents, or dependent children, for example), you will find that besides trying to maintaining balance in your own life, you must also take into consideration the goals of your family members.

As you ponder your future, you need to realize that pursuing your dreams may necessitate choices. Do not underestimate the sacrifices and work required to achieve your objectives. You may have to make difficult and sometimes painful choices between work, self, and home interests. Before starting your journey, honestly ask yourself whether you are willing to live with the physical, financial, and emotional costs involved. What price are you willing to pay to achieve everything you want out of life?

You may notice that while you are working on your lifestage plan you will also have to make assumptions regarding your career, lifestyle, health, and financial circumstances. If things turn out better than you assumed, great! If one or more of your assumptions turns out to be wrong, no problem. You will simply need to return to the applicable objective on your lifestage plan, make the appropriate changes, and charge ahead once again.

Exercise
Write Your Lifestage Plan

This will *not* be a one-time, permanent document. Don't get hung up on making all the details of your plan perfect in the first draft. If you get stuck, look back at the "Sampling of Lifestage Ideas" at the beginning of this chapter and at the thoughts you wrote down in the "Preliminary Planning" exercise. This may
Continued on page 84

Exercise: Write Your Lifestage Plan

Continued from page 83

seem like a daunting task, but it is really quite simple, and you'll be amazed at how much your lifestage plan will help you down the road. Just follow the steps outlined here:

1. Gather together several sheets of blank paper. On the first sheet, write the title "My Balanced Plan for the Next Years" and today's date. Use this sheet for your "Life Overview." Then use the remaining sheets for the three spheres of influence: "Work," "Self," and "Home." For your planning horizon, take the number of years you think you have left in your current lifestage or the number of years until the occurrence of an anticipated major life change event (for example, job change, graduation, marriage, child graduating from college, retirement). This will probably be somewhere between three and ten years.

2. Create a column on the left side of the paper and title it "Key Result Areas." Going down the column, write in your own customized key result areas for your three spheres of influence. Leave several blank horizontal lines for each key result area.

3. To the right of your list of key result areas, you are going to answer the following questions for each key result area:

STARTING POINT
Where am I now?

Here you will describe your opinion of yourself and your current situation, as accurately and honestly as you can. For example (in the personal finances key result area):
I overspend using credit cards, now owe $6,000.

SELF-ASSESSMENT
How do I feel about my current situation?

Write in a one-word description.

Happy — You don't need to change a thing.

Pretty good — You probably don't need to change a thing.

Neutral — You might want to consider a change.

Not that great — You should make a change.

Unhappy — You should change as soon as possible.

OBJECTIVE
What are my primary objectives in this key result area?

Look back at the objectives you wrote in the last exercise. Then look ahead at your situation at the end of this planning period if everything goes well for you between now and then. Are all of your objectives realistic? Concentrate on those that you could describe as your primary objectives for each key result area.

Get rid of debt, pay off entire credit balance each month.

PLAN
What must I do to get there?

Describe the actions you need to take (or the attitude and behavior changes you need to make) to meet your primary objective in each key result area for this planning period.

Pay off debt @ $500 plus interest each month, spend less.

DEADLINE
When would I like to get there?

Set a realistic deadline for achieving each objective.

Be out of debt by December 31.

REWARD
What will be my reward for getting there?

When you achieve your primary objective, how will you reward yourself and those who helped you get there?

I'll take my wife out to a candlelight dinner.

Now go to the quality checklist on pages 89–90.

My Balanced Plan for the Next Five Years
January 15, 19XX

LIFE OVERVIEW

Starting Point	My life is out of balance
Self-Assessment	Unhappy
Objective	Find a way to balance work and home life
Plan	Develop a balanced lifestage plan
Deadline	February 1
Reward	Take family on weekend vacation

Key Result Areas	WORK	
Acme Co. Overview	Starting Point	We don't have a clear picture of our niche in the marketplace
	Self-Assessment	Unhappy
	Objective	Find a niche that only we can uniquely fill in our market
	Plan	Develop a strategic plan for company
	Deadline	March 15
	Reward	Recognition from board of directors
Financial Data & Control	Starting Point	Expenses consistently exceed projections
	Self-Assessment	So so
	Objective	Find ways to balance budget
	Plan	Tighten expenditure controls to match forecasts
	Deadline	June 30
	Reward	Bonus to all team members

Figure 3.2
Sample first draft of a lifestage plan

Key Result Areas	WORK (continued)	
Productivity & Quality	Starting Point	Productivity is high, but quality is slipping
	Self-Assessment	So so
	Objective	Maintain productivity while improving quality
	Plan	Set up stricter quality control programs
	Deadline	December 31
	Reward	Year-end celebration party
Human Resources	Starting Point	Excessive absenteeism due to work-family conflicts
	Self-Assessment	Unhappy
	Objective	Reduce absenteeism by 50 percent
	Plan	Implement flex-time, job sharing, and day care programs
	Deadline	April 15
	Rewards	I would feel good about it Recruiting advantage
Customer Relations	Starting Point	We generate too few leads
	Self-Assessment	Unhappy
	Objective	Improve lead generation by 300 percent
	Plan	Develop, test, and implement a lead generation program
	Deadline	April 30
	Reward	Increased sales = increased bonus!

Continued on page 88

Key Result Areas	SELF	
Self-Development	Starting Point	I'm frustrated because I can't keep up with reading load
	Self-Assessment	Unhappy
	Objective	Double my reading speed
	Plan	Enroll in speed-reading course & practice daily
	Deadline	August 31, speed doubled
	Reward	1 week in Hawaii
Health & Fitness	Starting Point	10 pounds overweight, feel sluggish
	Self-Assessment	So so
	Objective	Permanently lose 10 pounds, get in shape
	Plan	Join health club, exercise 3 times per week, eat better
	Deadline	May 15, lost 10 pounds
	Reward	New wardrobe for summer
	HOME	
Personal Finances	Starting Point	I overspend using credit cards, now owe $6000
	Self-Assessment	Unhappy
	Objective	Get rid of debt, pay off credit cards each month
	Plan	Spend less, pay off $500 + interest each month
	Deadline	December 31
	Reward	A candlelight dinner for two

Figure 3.2 (continued)
Sample first draft of a lifestage plan

Key Result Areas	HOME	
Family & Lifestyle	Starting Point	I feel guilty for not spending more time with spouse and kids
	Self-Assessment	Unhappy
	Objective	Increase quality time with family to 10 hours per week
	Plan	Improve time management by sche-uling 10 specific hours each week
	Deadline	June 1
	Reward	One guilt-free game of golf each month with my friends
Friends & Community	Starting Point	Happily involved with church affairs
	Self-Assessment	Happy
	Objective	Help church to collect $10,000 for new roof
	Plan	Chair fundraising effort
	Deadline	October 1
	Reward	Gratitude of congregation

Quality Check

As you work on your lifestage plan, continue to do the SMARTER test on your objectives. Does each objective have the following characteristics?

Specific
Measurable
Achievable
Results-Oriented
Timebounded
Exciting
Readily Available

If the answer is "no" for any given objective, revise your plan. This system works only if you are truly committed to all of your objectives. In addition, check to make sure that each objective is in harmony with your core motivators.

Remember that specific, measurable, and achievable objectives give meaning and purpose to life, and your dail challenge is to spend your time in a way that is helping you fulfill your vision. You'll know that you have a good lifestyle plan when you can say

Exercise
Reality Check

Take a helicopter overview of your lifestage plan to make sure that the objectives for each key result area are realistic. Each objective needs to be achievable by itself, but as a group they also need to be achievable. Are you being realistic about how much you can accomplish within the chosen time frame? And are your objectives within each key area in balance with those in the other key result areas?

To ensure that your lifestage plan is realistic, ask yourself the following questions:

- Do I know exactly where I want to go in each sphere of influence in my life?
- Is my lifestage plan balanced to my satisfaction, without any significant conflicts between work, self, and home?
- Does each one of my objectives support my vision, my motivators, and my purpose in life?
- Is each one of my objectives realistic?

If the answer to any of these questions is "no," you need to return to the applicable objective and reconsider how you will rewrite it until it fits.

to yourself, "I believe that I can really do this. Now I truly have something to look forward to — at work, at home, and for myself! I can't wait to get started!"

Balance Test

Balance (like life itself) is never perfect. Nor is it permanent. Each one of us defines balance in our own unique way, and what you consider to be a life in balance may be the opposite for someone else. Only you can sense when the spheres of influence in your life have reached an acceptable state of balance.

Changes tend to throw you out of balance, but remember that not all changes are catastrophes. Some lead to improvements in the quality of life, some require minor adjustments to a few objectives. As Sue Shellenbarger noted recently in her *Wall Street Journal* "Work & Family" column, "There is, many would say, no right or wrong way to integrate work and family. There are only more or less costly ways in terms of career, relationships, or health."[8]

Consider your life to be in an acceptable balance when you are happy and fulfilled most of the time, and when you don't feel like you are neglecting anything or anyone of importance in your life. In other words, you're probably in balance when you know within yourself that you're not focusing on any one of your three spheres of influence at the expense of one or both of the others.

Of course, there are times when you simply must work long hours at the office or stay away from home on business for several nights at a time. During those times you can't help but give less than ideal attention to your self and your home life. At other times you may find yourself neglecting your work because you have a family problem or you are sick. During these times you can use your common sense to temporarily focus on the immediate need while realizing that you will soon get back into a normal balance. These kinds of changes can be compensated for with minor and temporary adjustments to your lifestage plan.

Some changes, though, demand more attention. When unhappiness and a feeling of a lack of fulfillment persist until your life seems to be permanently out of balance, you will know that this is more serious. Perhaps you have a new baby at home, and by the third month you realize that your new responsibilities as a parent will place unforeseen demands on your time for the next eighteen years. Or perhaps your mother has died after a long illness; you spent so much time caring for her while she was ill that by the third month after the funeral you realize you suddenly have a lot of spare time. In both examples, you obviously have reached the point where you need to revise your lifestage plan until you again are satisfied with the attention given to each of your spheres of influence.

In the worst cases, a full-blown crisis — perhaps some unpredictable catastrophe (an earthquake, a fire, an automobile accident) — brings activities in all three spheres of influence to a halt. Merely adjusting a few objectives won't work. In Chapter 4, you'll find more information about how to manage such major life crises, including how to redefine your vision, motivators, and purpose in life.

Exercise
Test Your Balance

A sense of balance is very personal. With your lifestage plan adjusted so it is balanced, you should be able to live each and every day without creating unacceptable levels of stress.

Our colleague, the psychotherapist and noted author Dr. John Baucom, inspired us to develop the following self-examination for determining the status of your balance level. A number of the items are from his book, *The Elvis Syndrome.*[9]

Your first time through this test will create a baseline for your current balance level. As you take the test at later periods in your life, you will begin to have an indication of whether you have achieved a greater sense of stability or you are losing balance. That discovery may be the trigger you need to make changes. Remember, not all changes are caused by external forces.

Directions

Give yourself a grade for each of the items listed below. Assign grades as follows:

4 (A)   Something you do consistently
3 (B)   Above-average performance
2 (C)   Sometimes yes, sometimes no
1 (D)   Something you rarely do
0 (F)   Something you never do

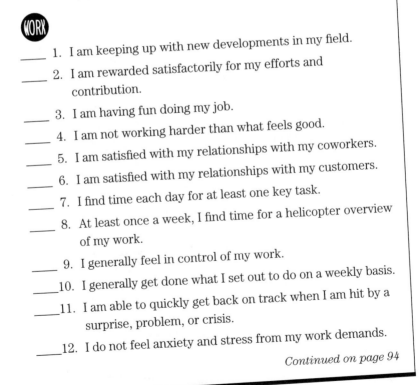

_____ 1. I am keeping up with new developments in my field.

_____ 2. I am rewarded satisfactorily for my efforts and contribution.

_____ 3. I am having fun doing my job.

_____ 4. I am not working harder than what feels good.

_____ 5. I am satisfied with my relationships with my coworkers.

_____ 6. I am satisfied with my relationships with my customers.

_____ 7. I find time each day for at least one key task.

_____ 8. At least once a week, I find time for a helicopter overview of my work.

_____ 9. I generally feel in control of my work.

_____10. I generally get done what I set out to do on a weekly basis.

_____11. I am able to quickly get back on track when I am hit by a surprise, problem, or crisis.

_____12. I do not feel anxiety and stress from my work demands.

Continued on page 94

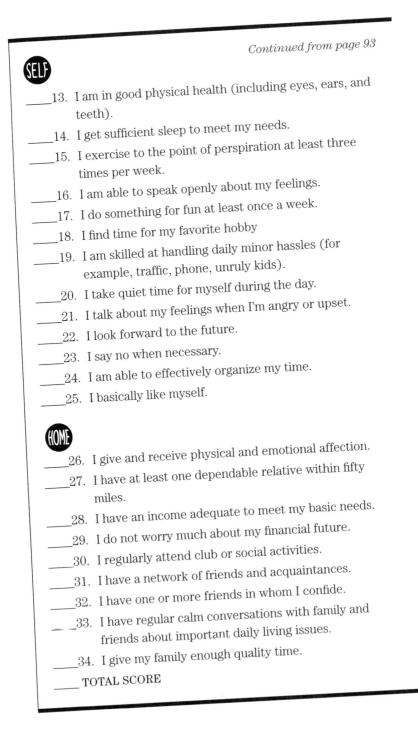

Continued from page 93

SELF

____13. I am in good physical health (including eyes, ears, and teeth).

____14. I get sufficient sleep to meet my needs.

____15. I exercise to the point of perspiration at least three times per week.

____16. I am able to speak openly about my feelings.

____17. I do something for fun at least once a week.

____18. I find time for my favorite hobby

____19. I am skilled at handling daily minor hassles (for example, traffic, phone, unruly kids).

____20. I take quiet time for myself during the day.

____21. I talk about my feelings when I'm angry or upset.

____22. I look forward to the future.

____23. I say no when necessary.

____24. I am able to effectively organize my time.

____25. I basically like myself.

HOME

____26. I give and receive physical and emotional affection.

____27. I have at least one dependable relative within fifty miles.

____28. I have an income adequate to meet my basic needs.

____29. I do not worry much about my financial future.

____30. I regularly attend club or social activities.

____31. I have a network of friends and acquaintances.

____32. I have one or more friends in whom I confide.

____33. I have regular calm conversations with family and friends about important daily living issues.

____34. I give my family enough quality time.

____ TOTAL SCORE

To determine your current balance level, divide your total score by 34 (the number of questions). There is no passing or failing grade. Some people can tolerate more stress and instability in their lives than others. Likewise, at some stages of your life you will need a higher level of balance than at others.

Use this score as a relative indication of your balance level. Periodically retake the self-exam and compare your scores to see if your balance has improved or taken a turn for the worse.

C H A P T E R   4

Living Your Plan

Motivation is what gets you started. Habit is what keeps you going.

— Jim Ryun[1]

IF YOU HAVE COMPLETED the exercises in the first three chapters of this book, you are well on your way to creating greater success, balance, and happiness in your life. But there's still one more step to take. You need a system for implementing your lifestage plan. In this chapter, you'll find an effective life management system that will help you accomplish the following:

- Give you an overview of your three spheres of influence (work, self, and home).
- Motivate you to work toward fulfilling your vision and your purpose in life.
- Enable you to achieve your objectives through the creation of realistic action plans.
- Plan for change and thereby generate viable options and better control.
- Create and maintain effective balance of the three spheres of influence, no matter what happens.

For most of us, balancing work with family and home life is an ongoing challenge. Creating a viable lifestage plan requires insight, judgment, and the ability to see the big picture, but implementing that plan requires a proactive use of the basic building block of life — time.

One Second at a Time

Our costliest expenditure is time.
— Theophrastus (c. 370–287 B.C.)[2]

Time is the continuum along which we track our progress through life. Time is the common denominator we all share, and every one of us decides each day how to spend it — or waste it. As a nonrenewable resource, time can't be put into a savings account, to be used at a later date. And even worse, once spent, time is gone forever. "Lost time is never found again," according to an old proverb.[3] Since we never get the chance to relive yesterday, we can only look to the future.

More time can't be manufactured, but the time you have left can be better managed. How? *The answer is obvious — plan well, prioritize daily, and then take action accordingly* — and this is truly the only way. Even if you have very little control over what you do during your working hours, you still control the rest of your day, which is the majority of your time. You need to ask yourself some basic questions: What are you doing with your time after you get off work? *Are you wasting your time or are you using it to improve your life?*

Some people say "I don't have the time for that," when actually what they're saying is that something else is more important. *We all find time to do what we really want* — whether it's working, pursuing a hobby, or spending time with our family. The trick to finding success, happiness, and fulfillment without time pressure is to determine what you really want out of life and then allocate time to concentrate on just that! What we teach is truly "beyond time management." It is life management.

Others may say, "There just isn't enough time in the day to

accomplish everything." Obviously they haven't thought about what's really important to them. They are trying to keep too many unimportant balls in the air at the expense of those that really matter. They have not prioritized their objectives.

For most adults, the predominant source of stress is frustration with attempting to balance the time demands of work and the responsibilities of home life. The key to achieving balance is to look at the various elements of your lifestage plan as a whole rather than as a group of various commitments. When you do this you will have a better understanding of how changing the commitment to any one element affects all the others. In the end, the only way to effectively managing your time is to make difficult choices, to set limits on the number of hours you are willing to work while reserving some time for family, recreational activities, and self-improvement.

You have an obligation to yourself to make the most of what you can control: today and each day hereafter for the rest of your life. Whether you vegetate in front of a television set or use your time to pursue your dreams, the choice is in your hands. Waste your time and you will probably waste your life; use your time wisely and you can achieve your vision and fulfill your life purpose.

Managing Time for Optimum Results

Time is the scarcest resource, and unless it is managed nothing else can be managed.
— Peter Drucker[4]

You should always be asking yourself: What is the best use of my time right now? Is what you're doing today getting you closer to where you want to be tomorrow? If your answer is "no," then you should make a change. If you are reluctant to change, examine closely the consequences of not changing as well as the potential benefits that will come with change.

Since you've read this far, we're assuming that you have written out your vision statement, a list of your motivators, your purpose in life, and a personalized list of key result areas. You also should have written a lifestage plan that includes objectives for each key result area, with each objective worded in such a way that is measurable and timebounded.

At this point, you need to have your personalized list of key result areas in front of you. The next step is to develop a specific action plan for each objective on this list. This will help you overcome the single greatest barrier to achieving success in any area: starting to move from where you are to where you want to be. Any journey begins with one small step, and each subsequent step reduces the distance between where you are and your goal.

Some people get so discouraged at this point that they don't even try to bridge that gap, while others give up before reaching their goal. Do yourself a great favor: Don't be like that. Instead of walking away from the challenge, break it up into manageable bites. Instead of being overwhelmed by the magnitude of your objectives, think of them as consisting of a series of steps or sub-objectives.

We call these sub-objectives key tasks. These are the specific steps you need to take to meet your responsibilities and complete the projects in each key result area. An action plan is merely a series of key tasks that can be completed one at a time. Just like climbing a mountain one step at a time, you realize your objectives one task at a time. When you give each key task in the action plan a deadline, you end up with a simple and methodical planning process that is designed to lead you toward completion of your objectives. Figure 4.1 summarizes the process.

By breaking each objective down into manageable key tasks, effective planning easily and systematically leads to the achievement of results. Day by day you simply allocate realistic blocks of time to work on the next key task for your high-priority objectives.

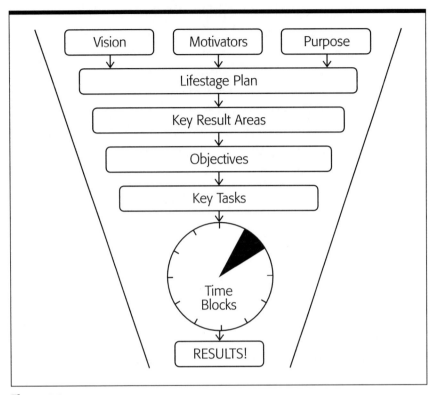

Figure 4.1
From vision to results via the Geodex success process

Here's how you do it:

1. Use a separate sheet of paper for each objective that is important to your success.

2. Identify the key result area(s) involved, write in the objective, and write today's date.

3. List the key tasks (action steps, sub-objectives, or project components) required to reach the objective.

4. Set a budget (time and/or money) and indicate target dates for starting, reviewing, and completing each task.

5. To prevent problems, identify what might go wrong. Consider all relevant factors, including time, people involved, materials, money, quality, and quantity. Indicate what you need to do in each of these areas to prevent the problem from happening. (It is always better to be a problem preventer than a problem solver.)

6. Make a list of resources you will need to successfully complete each task (people, materials, money, and any others you can think of).

As you complete your action plans, organize them by key result area, and keep them all together in a binder or notebook. You don't have to complete all of them right now. Do those you consider most important and hold off on others until later. Two to five detailed plans at any given time is a comfortable amount for most people. Periodically take a helicopter overview. First scan over your vision, motivators, and purpose to reconfirm who you are. Then for each key result area, consider your objectives with matching action plans and deadlines. Ask yourself the following questions:

- Do I know exactly where I want to go?
- Will the tasks outlined on my action plans lead me in the direction I want to go?
- Are my deadlines realistic?

You will find that this simple process reaffirms your commitment and also quickly points out when a revision is needed. Notice, we say "when" revision is needed, because — like life itself — this is a process of constant refinement. As time goes by, your priorities will naturally change. As some goals are reached, others increase (or diminish) in importance.

When you are satisfied with your lifestage plan, your objectives, and your action plans, turn to your time planner and write in all the beginning, review, and deadline dates for each project.

ACTION PLAN

January 3, 19XX

Objective: Eliminate all my credit card debt (approx. $6000) by December 31 of this year.

Reward: A candlelight dinner for two on New Year's Eve.

Key Tasks	Who	(time/$)	Budget Start	Review	Deadline
1. Summarize last 12 months' spending	me	3 hours	Jan. 6		Jan. 21
2. Identify all extravagant or one-time spending	spouse	1 hour	Jan. 21	Jan. 22	Jan. 23
3. Create a realistic budget for next 12 months	me	1 hour	Jan. 24	Jan. 25	Jan. 26
4. Meet with spouse & family to agree on budget	me	1/2 hour	Jan. 26	Jan. 26	Jan. 26
5. Find lowest interest-rate credit card available	me	1 hour	Jan. 26		Jan. 28
6. Consolidate all debt onto new card	me	1/2 hour	Jan. 28		Jan. 30
7. Destroy all other cards	spouse	5 min.	Jan. 30		Jan. 30
8. Sell third car, use proceeds to pay down debt	me	5 hrs/$25	Jan. 25		Feb. 10
9. Pay minimum $500 per month on new card	me		monthly		
10. Debt eliminated!	me			monthly	Dec. 31

Figure 4.2
Sample action plan for the objective "Be out of debt by December 31"

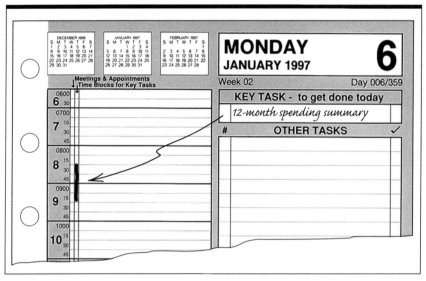

Figure 4.3
Target dates and time blocks for each key task are noted on a time planner

Exercise
Set Up a Life Management System

A life management system is like a combination of your mental coach, your helicopter, your compass, and your navigational charts. With it you can pursue many things simultaneously, whereas with your conscious mind alone, you can deal with only a few things at a time. A life management system will help you focus on your objectives while reminding you which step to take next.

More than 100,000 people are currently using the Geodex Life Management System, a binder-based tool designed for developing and implementing a lifestage plan. This system takes you through the Geodex success process, as outlined in Figure 4.1. For more information about this system, see Appendix 2 or call (800) 833-3030 and request more information. Mention this book when you call and we'll send you some life-planning tools free!

Finally (and this is crucial to your success), *begin the habit that separates high-achievers from everyone else: Do not let a single day go by without completing at least one of the key tasks that will lead toward the achievement of one of your high-priority objectives.* It has been our experience that most people complete no more than two or three key tasks in a typical week. The rest of their time is taken up by urgent but not important tasks, maintenance tasks, or time wasters that have little or no bearing on achieving their life objectives. It has been our experience that by scrupulously striving to complete one key task every day, most people will, in one bold stroke, double their productivity.

One key task every single day!

By following this simple self-management tip, you'll double your output and reach your objectives twice as fast as most of your contemporaries. This is a sure way to be a high achiever!

Planning as a Process

The best way to predict your future is to plan it.
— General Douglas MacArthur[5]

Just as having a regular maintenance schedule helps keep your car running at its peak performance, you should regularly give your lifestage plan a tune-up. To put it another way, look at your road map once in a while to make sure that you're still going in the right direction. Your lifestage plan is your navigational aide and it should not be a static document. Use pencil and allow for erasing out one objective and writing in another.

Don't make the common mistake of painstakingly writing out your lifestage plan and then filing it away with no intention of ever reviewing or revising it. Scan your plan at least monthly (if not weekly) to make sure that it still fits you and your life situation. While you have it in front of you, review your vision statement, your list of motivators, and your life purpose to see if they still fit. Motivators don't usually change with time, but their priority might and this could, in turn, influence your purpose and indicate a need to set new goals. Many of our clients report that they like to do a helicopter overview of their lifestage plan while traveling, when they're free from everyday stresses and responsibilities.

Whenever you see that you are seriously deficient in one or more spheres of influence in your life, repeat the planning process. Rewrite your vision, reexamine your list of motivators. Make adjustments in your objectives until your life is again in balance. Ambivalence is a common human characteristic, and many people struggle to find the most appropriate foundation for their lifestage plan. Once you've found yours, guard it jealously. You will have a natural competitive advantage.

Techniques for Achieving Success

There are no secrets to success. It is the result of preparation, hard work, learning from failure.
— General Colin L. Powell[6]

Life is not always easy, and the road to success is often paved with potholes and detours. Change your perspective: Look at these challenges as opportunities for producing positive changes rather than as obstacles making your life difficult. Be stubborn and determined. Don't take "no" for an answer. Create a can-do attitude that tells the world every problem has a solution and it's your challenge to find it — and you will find it. When the road gets rough, try to remember our seven simple and proven techniques for achieving success in a world of many opportunities and constant change:

1. Expect and visualize the best outcome.

2. Choose your battles.

3. Look for opportunities.

4. Get moving.

5. Take risks.

6. Don't be afraid of failure.

7. Don't give up.

1. Expect and visualize the best possible outcome.

> *Think you can, [or] think you can't. Either way, you'll be right.*
>
> — Henry Ford[7]

Expectancy and visualization are two of the greatest untapped forces in the universe, and their beauty lies in both their simplicity and abundance. In our experience they represent two-thirds of realization, with the last third being purposeful action. In both of our personal lives and professional careers, we have often used the incredible powers of expectancy and visualization in numerous challenging situations to literally predetermine the desired outcome.

Expectancy

To practice expectancy you must have a deep belief in a specific outcome. Herein lies the power of expectancy, and what sets it apart from wishful thinking is the definite belief that no power in existence can prevent the fulfillment of your expected outcome.

When you set out toward your goals, do you really expect to succeed? Most people don't! Expect your desired outcome just as much as you expect to wake up tomorrow morning when you go to bed tonight. That is expectancy, and it's much more than positive thinking. It's about not letting even one negative thought pass through your mind. It embraces determination and enthusiasm tempered with sincerity and integrity.

It's easy to wish for something while knowing you will never get it. Expectancy is different. If you don't expect to accomplish something, then how can you hope to accomplish it? What you think about in life is what you're going to get, so think great things!

Visualization

As you have already learned in Chapter 2, creating and expressing a vision of your desired future can be a powerful stimulus for action. It is nothing more than applied expectancy. Visualization stimulates your determination, enthusiasm, and resourcefulness; it inspires your imagination. Envision your desires as already accomplished. Think about them often. Take definite, determined action, and all of a sudden (sometimes when you least expect it) you will actually see the fulfillment of your goals in life.

The techniques of expectancy and visualization are easy to apply. For example, each morning those in sales should expect their prospective customers to need their product or service. Today they should see their prospects' needs and then visualize both the sales presentation and the product in use by the prospect to satisfy those needs.

Each morning sit down for a moment and quietly visualize the things you desire to happen that day. Expect that they will come true. Realize that everything you desire to happen is only the visible outpouring of your own consciousness. Then take definite action with that expectancy constantly in your mind.

2. Choose your battles.

Pick battles big enough to matter, small enough to win.
— Jonathan Kozol[8]

Realize that you can only do so much. In particular, having too many objectives going at the same time can lead to stress and confusion. Eight current projects seem to be the maximum number most people can handle at any one time, and somewhere between two and five is much more comfortable. It's important to realize that you can only do so much.

The number of projects is not the only consideration, though. Try not to get buried in details or involved in problems that are out of your control. Set yourself up with at least a fighting chance of winning. Avoid situations where you have no realistic chance of achieving a positive outcome or realize that you are then only setting yourself up for the stress and anxiety of failure.

Many professionals are trained to choose their battles. Fire-fighters create a containment ring around an out-of-control forest fire. If the fire is in an inaccessible area or if they are short on manpower, they decide to let it burn itself out. A battlefield triage doctor must decide which wounded soldiers are savable with the available resources.

When you are feeling stressed out or under time pressure, you can use the same strategy. If you feel too exhausted to cook dinner and then clean up, consider ordering take-out or going out to eat. If you feel you need to spend more time with your family, consider skipping some social functions. If you want to work on your budget or converse with someone uninterrupted, consider letting your answering machine take calls for a while. Although working on this book was a high priority, Kim often chose to take his laptop computer home, where he could work uninterrupted and away from the distractions of a busy office, and Willy took his laptop to the cabin of his sailboat.

3. Look for opportunities.

To improve the golden moment of opportunity, and catch the good that is within our reach, is the great art of life.
— Samuel Johnson[9]

We often hear people complain that only a lucky few find success and happiness in life. We usually react to these people by telling them about the farmer from the old country:

> Once upon a time there was an old man who made a living on a small farm with the help of his only son and one horse. One day the horse ran away and disappeared up into the hills. When his neighbors pitied his bad luck and asked him how he would ever manage the farm with no horse, his only answer was "Who knows whether it's good luck or bad luck?"
>
> That evening, just before sunset, the villagers were surprised to see an entire herd of wild horses come down from the hills. Led by the farmer's horse, they ran right into his corral. The farmer's son quickly closed the gate and now the farmer had not just one but twelve horses. His neighbors envied his luck, saying, "Around here nobody else has more than one horse, but now you are so lucky you have twelve of them." His only response was "Who knows whether it's good luck or bad luck?"
>
> The next morning the farmer's son, a feisty young fellow, decided he'd try to ride the biggest of the wild horses. Although he was an experienced rider, the wild horse immediately threw him off and in the fall the farmer's son broke his hip. Once again the neighbors commented on the farmer's bad luck, saying, "This bad luck will put you out of business. There is no way you can run the farm and manage all these horses without your son." Once more he answered, "Who knows whether it's good luck or bad luck?"
>
> That same night a military horn was heard in the distance, and before long a warlord entered the village and conscripted all the young men — except for the farmer's son, who

was in bed with a body cast. Now the neighbors wailed, "Why is it that you are so lucky? Everyone else has had their son drafted, but yours was not." And once more his answer was, "Who knows whether it's good luck or bad luck?"

This story goes on and on, as long as those who are listening will allow us to go. In our family, among our employees, and with our clients, all you have to do is say: "Remember the old farmer..." and immediately any contemplation of good or bad luck is put in the proper perspective.

> *You don't just luck into things... you build step by step,*
> *whether as friendships or opportunities.*
> — Barbara Bush[10]

There is no such thing as luck. Good luck is when a prepared mind meets the right opportunity. Bad luck is when your lack of preparation leads you to react inappropriately or fail to react at all. It is no coincidence that the harder you work, the luckier you get.

How do you increase your "luck" quotient?

- Don't be afraid of change. Be prepared to meet both predictable and unpredictable changes.

- Look for opportunities in every situation. Most opportunities don't come to you, you come to them.

Many opportunities are disguised as change, stress, and turmoil. Surrendering to the inevitability of change will be most beneficial to your sanity and prosperity, for within change lies opportunity. Zen masters and those skilled in the martial arts have a great respect for the power of submission as a positive force. They know that to yield — to give in to a situation — often provides the only path to mastery of that situation. They speak of going with change or with an opposing force rather than against it.

The strongest trees bend with the wind or they break. Go with the flow. Use the force of opposing power to your advantage by letting its strength become yours. No matter what happens, remember your vision, and make sure your actions are in alignment with your motivators and your purpose. A wonderful Oriental proverb summarizes this concept: "Once you start moving in the direction of your destiny, your destiny begins to move toward you." Be proactive!

4. Get moving.

You miss 100 percent of the shots you never take.
— Wayne Gretsky's coach[11]

Every day you choose how you spend your time and resources. To have any chance of success in life, you must step up to bat and swing. Sometimes you'll swing and miss, sometimes you'll get a base hit, but sooner or later — if you keep swinging — you'll hit a home run. Remember, in professional baseball the players who hit the most home runs also lead in strikeouts. In the game o life, winners don't wait for an invitation to succeed. They make it happen.

The average American adult spends more than two hours per day watching television. Over the course of a lifetime, this amounts to roughly six solid years! Imagine how many of your objectives you could accomplish during six years of completing key tasks! Look for other ways to reallocate wasted time. Move closer to your place of business and spend less time commuting to work, or take a new job closer to home. Drive an old car so you can afford to buy a house. Cut back on entertainment or dining out so you can meet your goal for retirement savings.

How you spend your time, energy, and resources is up to you. Your lifestage plan won't become reality until you get to work on it. Without continuous and diligent work on your part, your dreams will never be realized. A wise man once said that the only place success comes before work is in the dictionary!

Don't Procrastinate

Even if you're on the right track, you'll get run over if you just sit there.

— Will Rogers[12]

Procrastination is the greatest time-robber there is. Within procrastination lies the graveyard of opportunity. But it's easy to avoid this scourge of high achievement if you follow our anti-procrastination tips:

- Share your lifestage plan with others. Making your intentions public helps deepen your commitment to success.

- Actively imagine success and continue to visualize positive results.

- Before you start working on any given objective, gather all the information you will need.

- Divide and conquer. Divide your objectives into key tasks and conquer them one at a time.

- "Well begun is half done." Take that first step, it is usually the most difficult.

- Do the easy things first. This builds momentum. Or do the hardest things first. This makes the home stretch very easy.

- Be sure that the rewards are motivating to you.

- Post a progress chart so you can see your successes.

5. Take risks.

The men who have done big things are those who were not afraid to attempt big things, who were not afraid to risk failure in order to gain success.

— B. C. Forbes[13]

Throughout the history of our country, immigrants have risked losing family, friends, and familiarity (and oftentimes their lives as well) for the opportunity of a better life. In today's hostile business climate, more and more people are at risk of being down-sized out of a job, but those who are prepared don't just wait for the inevitable. They take a chance and make a change. Any successful salesman will tell you that to succeed you must be willing to face the risk of rejection by every prospect.

We all tend to gravitate toward what is comfortable and secure, but to get ahead, the comfort zone must be left behind. It's easy to get stuck in routines, but to get ahead it is necessary to try something different, open a new door, try some wild idea. Remember the old English proverb: Nothing ventured, nothing gained!

6. Don't be afraid of failure.

> *Failure... is, in a sense, the highway to success, inasmuch as every discovery of what is false leads us to seek earnestly after what is true, and every fresh experience points out some form of error which we shall afterward carefully avoid.*
>
> — John Keats[14]

Thomas Edison experienced thousands of failures (and also accidentally set fire to his laboratory several times) before he succeeded in inventing the incandescent light bulb. But how did he describe this? "I didn't fail ten thousand times. I successfully eliminated, ten thousand times, material and combinations that wouldn't work."[15] What a great example of persistence and the stubborn willingness to endure setback after setback. He didn't give up and was ultimately rewarded for his efforts.

A child falls hundreds of times while learning to walk, but never gives up. Over and over, toddlers crawl, grab something on which to pull up, step away, and fall. A child doesn't think of falling as failure, whereas many adults become timid and quit an activity after only one attempt. Many more never start for fear of failure!

Fear of making mistakes will prevent you from learning. Failure, on the other hand, is the master educator. On your journey through life, you will most certainly experience some failure. You will meet many obstacles and have numerous setbacks. Accept failure and mistakes as part of the success process. We encourage you to fail quickly, fail intelligently, and learn from your mistakes. Reexamine your goals, adjust your course, then move on.

7. Don't give up.

Life is either a daring adventure or nothing. To keep our faces toward change and behave like free spirits in the presence of fate is strength undefeatable.
— Helen Keller[16]

Persistence is one of the true keys to success in life, but it must be used judiciously. Repeating the same failed actions while expecting a different result is not persistence, it's stupidity! Like Thomas Edison, you need to generate and test alternative solutions to the challenges you face. Persistence is trying many different approaches until you find the one that works best.

Many people know where they want to end up, but they can't figure out all the intermediate action steps necessary to get there. Our advice to these people is to remember that the road to success is never straight. Your map doesn't need to be accurate down to the smallest tenth of a mile. It's more important to take the first step. As the terrain unfolds before you, the next steps will become more apparent, revealing themselves as your plan unfolds. As you move closer toward your objective, the approximation process of making mid-course decisions and adjustments is ultimately what will allow you to realize your vision of success.

Exercise
Life Satisfaction Test

As a measure of your enthusiasm for life, this test can help you determine whether or not you are satisfied when you retire to your bed in the evening and when you wake up in the morning. Every day, answer these questions:

- Did I sleep well?
- Did I awake with a feeling of excitement about the day ahead of me?

If you fall asleep with a feeling of contentment and if you wake up with a feeling of eager anticipation for what's to come, then you are undoubtedly happy with the balance in your life and the progress you're making toward your goals. You are on the path of success.

If you toss and turn all night because of the stress in your life, if you feel like pulling the sheets over your head each morning with a wish that the day to go away, then you are probably leading an unhappy life and in need of a new plan for success.

Responding to Crisis

> *The ultimate measure of a man is not where he stands in moments of comfort and convenience, but where he stands at times of challenge and controversy.*
> — Martin Luther King, Jr.[17]

Crisis tends to be imposed unpredictably from the external world. But some very difficult times are based on inner turmoil, when the stress is self-inflicted or caused by an unwillingness to take action. Finally we reach a trigger point and make a change. This generally occurs when the pain of not changing is greater than the fear (or anticipated pain) of changing.

In the midst of crisis, we often feel entirely lost. We no longer know where we're going or what we want out of life, and many of us respond inappropriately by shutting down or tuning out entirely. Whenever traumatic or unpredictable events occur, they must be dealt with immediately. The challenge is being able to react in a controlled and effective manner, to maintain your balance, and to be able to go on achieving your vision.

In fact, things may not be as bad as you think. If you calmly and deliberately approach crises or life-changing events with a detached view, you will find it easier to put the issue in perspective. Once you can see more clearly, you can more easily move on to action that is appropriate and effective, and to reestablishing balance in your life.

We are going to suggest a crisis management plan as a way of proactively dealing with crisis, but your thoughts and attitudes are as important to success in this area as your actions. Before you begin to act, take a moment to check your attitude against the following suggestions:

- Expect to solve the problem. Expectations of success often generate success.
- Visualize what you want. Form a clear picture in your mind of your future with the crisis behind you.
- Take the attitude that you are going to resolve the issue. Assume that every question has an answer. Persist until that answer is found.
- Accept responsibility for your actions, and don't blame others.
- Be prepared to cut your losses. It is better to write off hopeless situations and move on to the next challenge.

The ultimate objective is to come out on top: to win and succeed through change instead of allowing change to create chaos in your life. You can't change whatever happened to precipitate this crisis, but you can shift your focus to the future. This will allow you to revise your lifestage plan to accommodate the changes and to reshape your vision for the future. This is also essential if you are to continue to be prepared to deal with any subsequent crises.

Exercise
Manage Your Crisis

When you find yourself in the midst of a high-impact crisis or life-change event, take some time to figure out exactly what is happening and how your current lifestage plan is going to be affected. This will put you in a better position to recreate your lifestage plan and go on with a productive life.

Part 1: Situation Analysis

1. Exactly what happened?

2. Why did this happen?

3. How do I feel about this life-change event or crisis?
   Answer the following questions with a "yes" or "no."

   - Is it over?
   - Can I live with it?
   - Is it out of my hands?
   - Am I capable of ignoring it?

     If you answered "yes" to these questions, you're ready to reexamine lifestage plan and make any necessary adjustments caused by the crisis.

     If you answered "no" to these questions, continue working through the questions that follow. Try to ignore what you can't control or do anything about. Be prepared to cut your losses. Some situations are best written off so that you can move on to the next challenge.

4. What do I stand to lose because of this?

5. What is the opportunity in this event or crisis?

6. What is my desired outcome from this event or crisis?

Part 2: Solutions

7. Evaluate alternative ways to deal with this change event. (Do this for each alternative you can imagine.)

   • Description

   • Pro

   • Con

   • Ranking

   The solution to a crisis is seldom clear-cut. Carefully weigh the pros and cons, then pick the alternative that you intuitively feel is the best one for you. (Often, that will be the one you think of first after having slept on the problem.)

8. Decide on your preferred solution, then proceed to write out a specific objective with a detailed action plan for dealing with this particular life challenge.

9. Now act, take some quick action. Try to quickly regain some stability by assigning yourself some short-term key tasks that you can quickly complete (and feel good about). Countless people have told us that simply doing some task — however small and seemingly insignificant at the time — that takes them closer to reaching a lifestage plan objective helped them get back on their feet and reoriented toward success. So, clear off your desk and pull out the working files. Write an outline or the first sentence. Organize your resources. Look up a phone number. Make one phone call. Meet one person. Focus on completing these easy tasks, record your progress, and reward yourself for your accomplishments. This will remind you that you're not helpless and that things are at least moving in the right direction.

10. If you still feel out of balance, simply repeat this process.

Don't give up, even if you feel that your life is just one crisis after another. Some people actually deal with crises every day — as part of their job description. Firefighters, police officers, physicians, plumbers, and computer repair technicians spend the majority of their working time dealing with other peoples' crises. As part of their training, they are taught to be detached and objective, and this enables them to handle one crisis after another with minimal stress.

If dealing with crises is a "normal" part of your day, use this proactive approach to reduce their impact upon your life and your stress level:

1. Build some slack time into your daily schedule so you will have the flexibility to deal with crises and other surprises.

2. Over a period of time, record all the crises that occur in your life and group them into common types and categories.

3. List ways each type of crisis could have been prevented, if at all.

4. For the ones that occur most often, develop standard solutions.

5. Brainstorm with your team (or family) to figure out better ways of responding to crises.

6. Routinely add a cushion of 20 percent or more to your time estimates for tasks that tend to be crisis-prone.

7. Take a few deep breaths or relax for 10 or 15 minutes before you attack the next crisis.

If this situation or the changes required have upset you so much that your entire life seems in turmoil and you have lost your sense of purpose and direction in life, then consider repeating some or all of the life overview thinking you have already done. Also, consider whether you shouldn't seek some help from your spouse, a trusted friend, or a professional counselor.

Now It's Up to You

To know what has to be done, then do it, comprises the whole philosophy of practical life.
— Sir William Osler[18]

We believe in the rocking chair principle: When you are so old that all you want to do is sit in a rocking chair on the front porch of your house, you shouldn't have any regrets about how you lived your life. Have big dreams while you are still able to chase them. Don't put off until tomorrow what you can begin today. Don't just sit there, do something! Life is too short to waste any of it.

There is a Latin expression for this: *Carpe diem.* Seize the day. Live each day to your fullest potential and you will never have any regrets. *Those who find success and happiness tend to have two characteristics: they make detailed plans and they have a strong bias for action.* They create their own futures. They don't live vicariously through others, and they don't wait for their ship to come in. They make it happen!

When all is said and done there are only two choices: go through life as a passenger who allows fate to dictate your route, or to become a pilot and accept the responsibility for taking charge of your life. Only the second way will you be able to achieve your full potential. As Willy likes to say, "Time is life — and it's passing. What are you waiting for?"

The successful application of the time-tested ideas and strategies found in this book will ultimately be your responsibility, as it should be. If you take a little bit of time each day to manage your life, you will be rewarded with success, happiness, and fulfillment beyond your wildest expectations.

Always remember: *You are not entitled to happiness and success. You have to work for it to make it happen.* The choice is now yours to make! It is your life, your initiative, and your opportunity. Take the first step on your journey toward greater happiness, fulfillment, and success, and all the rest will come that much easier. The ball is now in your court... Take charge of your life!

Notes

Chapter 1   The Challenge

1. Johann von Goethe, quoted in *The Fairview Guide to Positive Quotations* (Minneapolis: Fairview Press, 1993), p. 299.

2. Charles F. Kettering, quoted in *The Fairview Guide to Positive Quotations* (Minneapolis: Fairview Press, 1993), p. 301.

3. U.S. Bureau of Census, International Data Base as of 8/15/96. The "World PopClock" ticks away 24 hours a day, 365 days a year, on the World Wide Web (www.census.gov/ipc-bin/popclockw).

4. William Bridges, *Job Shift: How to Prosper in a Workplace* (Reading, MA: Addison-Wesley, 1994), p. 5.

5. Michael Hammer and James Champy, *Reengineering the Corporation: A Manifesto for Business Revolution* (New York: HarperBusiness, 1993).

6. From Population Council's 1995 report "Families in Focus: New Perspectives on Mothers, Fathers, and Children." Summary available at www.popcouncil.org.

7. Richard Saul Wurman, *Information Anxiety* (New York: Doubleday, 1989), p. 336.

8. Lyman Lloyd Bryson, quoted in *The Fairview Guide to Positive Quotations* (Minneapolis: Fairview Press, 1993), p. 309.

9. Alvin Toffler, *Future Shock* (New York: Random House, 1970), p. 4.

10. Serenity Prayer, used by 12-step programs (most notably Alcoholics Anonymous), first stanza of a prayer written by theologian Reinhold Niebuhr, D.D.

11. "New Hopes, New Dreams," *Time,* August 26, 1996, pp. 40–52. "To Stand and Raise a Glass," *Newsweek,* July 1, 1996, pp. 52–56.

12. "New Hopes, New Dreams," *Time,* August 26, 1996, p. 52.

13. Dr. Benjamin Spock, quoted in *The Fairview Guide to Positive Quotations* (Minneapolis: Fairview Press, 1993), p. 15.

14. Zig Ziglar, February 10, 1994, in San Francisco, California, at the Peter Lowe International Seminar "Success '94!" Zig Ziglar Corporation, 3330 Earhart, Suite 204, Carrolton, TX 75006, (800) 527-0306.

15. John Lennon and Paul McCartney, "Can't Buy Me Love," *The Compleat Beatles,* Vol. 1, 1962–1966 (New York: Bantam, 1981), pp. 224–227.

16. Henry David Thoreau, quoted in *The Fairview Guide to Positive Quotations* (Minneapolis: Fairview Press, 1993), p. 361.

Chapter 2 The Foundation

1. Plato, quoted in *The Fairview Guide to Positive Quotations* (Minneapolis: Fairview Press, 1993), p. 165.

2. Oliver Wendell Holmes, quoted in *Quotes and Quips* (Salt Lake City: Covey Leadership Center, 1993), p. 65.

3. Extensive research has been done on lifestages. Others have developed different life development models, some with fewer stages and others with more. The lifestages discussed in this book are the best compromise between completeness and

brevity. For a list of excellent books on lifestages and life planning, see "Selected References for Further Study" on page 131.

4. John Ruskin, quoted in *The Fairview Guide to Positive Quotations* (Minneapolis: Fairview Press, 1993), p. 291.

5. John F. Kennedy, speaking at the Joint Session of Congress, May 25, 1961, quoted in *Bartlett's Familiar Quotations,* 16th ed. (New York: Little, Brown, 1992), p. 741.

6. Martin Luther King, Jr., speaking at the Lincoln Memorial, Washington, D.C., August 28, 1963, quoted in *The New Book of Knowledge* (Danbury, CT: Grolier, 1988), p. 247.

7. Henry David Thoreau, *Walden,* or *Life in the Woods* (New York, Macmillan Collier Books, 1962), p. 31.

8. Lao-tzu, quoted in *The Fairview Guide to Positive Quotations* (Minneapolis: Fairview Press, 1993), p. 165.

9. Michel de Montaigne, quoted in *The Fairview Guide to Positive Quotations* (Minneapolis: Fairview Press, 1993), p. 351.

Chapter 3 The Planning Mode

1. David Sarnoff, quoted in *The Fairview Guide to Positive Quotations* (Minneapolis: Fairview Press, 1993), p. 354.

2. Consider seeking a professional counselor if you feel unable to let go of old problems. Without emotional baggage, you will cover much more ground on your journey in a more efficient and gratifying manner.

3. Benedetto Varchi (Italian poet and historian, c. 1502–1565), *L'Ercolano,* quoted in *The Manager's Book of Quotations* (Rockville, MD: American Management Association, 1989), p. 157.

4. Kim Norup and Willy Norup, *How to Balance Your Life in 90 Minutes or Less* (Sonoma, CA: Geodex International, 1995), p. 31.

5. Peter F. Drucker, *Managing for Results* (New York: Harper & Row, 1964).

6. Seneca, quoted in *Thoughts on the Business of Life* (Chicago: Triumph Books, 1992), p. 384.

7. Grenville Kleiser, quoted in *Peter's Quotations: Ideas for Our Time* (New York: Quill, 1977), p. 41.

8. Sue Shellenbarger, *Wall Street Journal,* "Work & Family," April 19, 1995, p. B1.

9. John Baucom, *The Elvis Syndrome: How to Avoid Death by Success* (Minneapolis, MN: Fairview Press, 1995), pp. 147–148. Adapted and reprinted with permission.

Chapter 4 Living Your Plan

1. Jim Ryun (with Mike Phillips), In *Quest of Gold: The Jim Ryun Story* (San Francisco: Harper & Row, 1984). In this inspirational biography, Jim Ryun describes his ongoing struggle to achieve balance in his life.

2. Theophrastus (c. 370–287 B.C.), quoted in *The International Thesaurus of Quotations* (New York: Crowell, 1970), 971:63.

3. Quoted in Herbert V. Prochnow, *The Toastmaster's Treasure Chest* (San Francisco: Harper & Row, 1979), p. 431.

4. Peter Drucker, quoted in Joe Griffith (ed.), *Speaker's Library of Business* (Englewood Cliffs, NJ: Prentice Hall, 1990), p. 335.

5. Attributed to General Douglas MacArthur, source unknown.

6. General Colin L. Powell, quoted in *The Fairview Guide to Positive Quotations* (Minneapolis: Fairview Press, 1993), p. 436.

7. Henry Ford, quoted in *The Fairview Guide to Positive Quotations* (Minneapolis: Fairview Press, 1993), p. 263.

8. Jonathan Kozol, quoted in *The Fairview Guide to Positive Quotations* (Minneapolis: Fairview Press, 1993), p. 312.

9. Samuel Johnson, quoted in *The Fairview Guide to Positive Quotations* (Minneapolis: Fairview Press, 1993), p. 460.

10. Barbara Bush, quoted in *The Fairview Guide to Positive Quotations* (Minneapolis: Fairview Press, 1993), p. 461.

11. Wayne Gretzky attributes this saying to one of his coaches, quoted in Joe Griffith (ed.), *Speaker's Library of Business* (Englewood Cliffs, NJ: Prentice Hall, 1990), p. 9.

12. Will Rogers, quoted in *Quotes & Quips* (Provo, Utah: Covey Leadership Center, 1993), p. 60.

13. B. C. Forbes, quoted in *The Fairview Guide to Positive Quotations* (Minneapolis: Fairview Press, 1993), p. 396.

14. John Keats, quoted in David McNally, *Even Eagles Need a Push: Learning to Soar in a Changing World* by David McNally (New York: Delacorte, 1990), p. 7.

15. Thomas Edison, quoted in Joe Griffith (ed.), *Speaker's Library of Business* (Englewood Cliffs, NJ: Prentice Hall, 1990), p. 119.

16. Helen Keller, *Let Us Have Faith* (1940), quoted in *International Thesaurus of Quotations* (New York: Crowell, 1970), 16:4.

17. Martin Luther King, Jr., quoted in *The Fairview Guide to Positive Quotations* (Minneapolis: Fairview Press, 1993), p. 532.

18. William Osler, quoted in *The Fairview Guide to Positive Quotations* (Minneapolis: Fairview Press, 1993), p. 422.

Glossary

action plan   See *key result plan.*

balance   The ideal situation where you feel good about the time and attention you give to the three spheres of influence (work, self, and home) in your life, and no one sphere is so dominant that you neglect the others.

Geodex   The name of a tool that enables you to manage your entire world (*geo*) systematically, with skill and *dex*terity.

happiness   The goal of lifestage planning: a state where you have few worries. Life is fun and satisfying because you are living "on purpose," with your vision and motivators as guides.

key result area   The main areas of performance and responsibility on which you must concentrate your efforts and resources in order to achieve your unique job-related and personal vision of success.

key result plan   A detailed, step-by-step action plan for achieving a specific objective related to one of your key result areas. Consists of a series of key tasks with specific time allocations, resource budgets, and deadlines.

key task A component of the key result plan, these are the individual action steps that must be carried out one at a time in order to achieve a given objective.

lifestage A relatively predictable stage of development during the course of a lifetime. The lifestage concept is based on the research conclusion that life is composed of a series of relatively stable stages of renewal, fulfillment, and structure building, with sometimes difficult transition periods between them. Each of these periods is a lifestage.

lifestage plan A comprehensive, results-oriented plan that states the objectives for each key result area of your current or upcoming lifestage.

mission See *purpose.*

motivators The principles you truly believe that motivate and influence your thoughts, choices, habits, and actions.

objective A written sentence describing specifically what you want to accomplish in a key result area and by when. The three components of the objective are answers to three questions: what? how much? and by when?

purpose Your best desciption of why you have been put on this earth and the direction you will take to achieve your vision while being guided by your motivators. Your purpose gives your life meaning; it is the ultimate reason for doing what you do each day.

spheres of influence The three primary areas of influence in your life: work, self, and home.

time planner The tool you use to plan, monitor, and control how you spend your time — typically a paper-based calendar system or a computer program.

values See *motivators.*

vision An inspiring image of your desired future; a concise description of your dream for who you would become, what you would do, and where you would do it — if everything went your way.

Selected Readings for Further Study

General Interest

Drucker, Peter F. *Management: Tasks, Responsibilities, Practices.* New York: Harper Business, 1993.

Drucker, Peter F. *Managing in Turbulent Times.* New York: Harper Business, 1993.

Peters, Tom. *Thriving on Chaos: Handbook for a Management Revolution.* New York: HarperCollins, 1989.

Townsend, Robert. *Further Up the Organization: How to Stop Management from Stifling People and Strangling Productivity.* New York: Knopf, 1984.

Stages of Life and Life Management

Chapman, Elwood N. *Comfort Zones: Planning Your Future.* Menlo Park: Crisp Publications, 1993.

Clifton, Donald O., and Nelson, Paula. *Soar with Your Strengths.* New York: Dell, 1996.

Hopson, Barrie. *Build Your Own Rainbow: A Lifeskills Workbook.* San Diego: Pfeiffer & Co., 1993.

Laslett, Peter. *A Fresh Map of Life: The Emergence of the Third Age.* Cambridge: Harvard University Press, 1991.

Levinson, Daniel J. *The Seasons of a Man's Life.* New York: Ballantine Books, 1986.

McNally, David. *Even Eagles Need a Push: Learning to Soar in a Changing World.* New York: Dell, 1994.

Sheehy, Gail. *Passages.* New York: Bantam, 1984.

Sheehy, Gail. *Pathfinders.* New York: Bantam, 1982.

Time Management and Personal Productivity

Bliss, Edwin C. *Getting Things Done.* New York: Bantam, 1984.

Drucker, Peter F. *The Effective Executive.* New York: Harper Business, 1993.

Drucker, Peter F. *Managing for Results.* New York: Harper Business, 1993.

Mackenzie, R. Alec. *The Time Trap.* New York: AMACOM, 1990.

Noe, John R. *Peak Performance Principles for High Achievers.* New York: Berkley Publishing Group, 1986.

Silver, Susan. *Organized to Be the Best!: New Timesaving Ways to Simplify and Improve How You Work.* Los Angeles: Adams Hall, 1995.

Winston, Stephanie. *The Organized Executive: A Program for Productivity — New Ways to Manage Time, Paper, and People.* New York: W. W. Norton, 1994.

Strategic and Action Planning

Brandt, Steven C. *Strategic Planning in Emerging Companies.* Reading, MA: Addison-Wesley, 1981.

Kepner, Charles H., and Benjamin B. Tregoe. *The New Rational Manager.* Princeton: Kepner-Tregoe, Inc., 1981.

Poza, Ernesto J. *Smart Growth: Critical Choices for Business Continuity and Prosperity.* San Francisco: Jossey-Bass, 1989.

Schaffer, Robert H., and Harvey A. Thomson. "Successful Change Programs Begin with Results." *Harvard Business Review* 70 (Jan.–Feb. 1992): 80–89.

Tregoe, Benjamin B., and John W. Zimmerman. *Top Management Strategy.* New York: Simon & Schuster, 1980.

Samples of Job-Related Key Result Areas

MOST PEOPLE QUICKLY CREATE their own, personalized set of key result areas. On the following pages you will find composite sets of key result areas that we have compiled for various professions and job titles. Read through these job-related key result areas for ideas on how to establish the best combination that together will cover all of your results-oriented responsibilities. Some of you may find that you need to combine descriptions from several job headings to adequately cover your responsibilities.

CEO/President/Partner/Proprietor
Board of Directors
Competition
Consultants
Key Accounts
Management Development
 & Succession
New Business
Physical Resources
Policies
Product Development
Profitability
Public Relations/Corporate Image
Public Responsibility
Quality Improvement
Return on Investments/Capital
Sources of Funds
Special Projects
Strategic Planning
Trade & Government Relations

Accounting/Financial Manager
Accounting Systems
Administrative Control
Banking & Liquidity Control
Budgeting

Client Service
Credit Control
Data Processing
Financial Control
Forecasts
Internal Audit & Reports
Legal & Tax Information
Professional Education
Quality Improvement
Work in Progress

Product Manager

Advertising/Sales Strategies & Plans
Market Information
Product Development & Mix
Product Knowledge & Information
Product/Service Image
Profitability & Budget Control
Quality Improvement

Project Manager/Engineer/Technical Supervisor

Budget Control
Current Project (A, B, C, …)
Miscellaneous Other Products
Product Development
Product/Service Knowledge
Quality Improvement
Technology
Work Methods & Techniques

Sales Manager

Advertising/Public Relations
Competition
Customer Mix
Customer Relations

Customer Service
Distribution Channels
Export
Key Accounts
New Markets
Personal Accounts
Pricing
Product Development
Product Mix
Sales Budget & Cost Control
Salespeople Effectiveness
Sales Policies
Sales Strategies
Sales Systems
Waste Control
Work in Progress
Work Methods

Training/Human Resources Development Manager

Current Training Programs
Indoctrination Programs
Internal Staff Coordination
Management Development Programs
Market/Product Knowledge
Organizational Development
Process Improvement
Prospective Training Programs
Training Budget
Training Materials & Facilities
Training Needs Assessment
Training Skills Techniques

Purchasing Agent/Manager

Financial Control/Budgets/Costs

Inventory Control
Potential Suppliers
Purchasing Policies
Purchasing Prices & Quantities
Quality Standards & Controls
Quotations & Orders in Progress
Supplier Relations & Contracts
Waste Control

Marketing Manager

Advertising/Promotion
   Effectiveness
Market Development
Marketing Policies
Marketing Strategies & Plans
Organizational Identity & Image
Product Development & Mix
Product/Service Knowledge
Quality Improvement

Personnel Manager

Career Planning
Employee Benefits
Industrial Relations
Management Development
   & Training
Staff Development
Needs Assessment
Organizational Development
Pensions
Personnel Policies
Personnel Records
Process Improvement
Recruitment/Selection
Union Relations
Wage & Salary Control

Public Relations/Information Manager

Crisis Management
Market Information
Media Relations
Media Selection List
Organizational Image & Identity
Product/Service Image
Public Relations Policies

Consultant in Private Practice

Advertising & Public Relations
Client Acquisition
Competition
Continuing Education
Current Projects
Daily & Client Time Records
Key Client (A, B, C, …)
Long-Range Planning
Market Information
Quality Improvement

Secretary/Staff Assistant

Communication Techniques
External Communication
Follow-Up Assignments
Internal Communication
Manager's Key Result Areas
   & Projects
Manager's Time Management
Meeting Arrangements
Office Equipment Maintenance
   & Service
Office Management
Process Improvement
Product/Service Knowledge

Travel Arrangements
Work Methods & Systems

Computer Programmer/Data Processing Manager

Computer Equipment
Manual Design Techniques
Process Improvement
Program (A, B, C, …)
Programming Languages
Programming Techniques
Research & Development

Store Manager/Retailer

Advertising & Public Relations
Budget Control
Campaigns/Clearance Sales
Competition
Coordination with Other
   Departments
Customer Service
Displays & Decorations
Facilities including Maintenance
Inventory Control & Turnover
Market Information
   (Customers/Competition)
Pricing
Product Knowledge
Product Mix & Range
Profitability
Purchasing
Quality Control
Security
Supplier Relations

Bank Manager

Branch/Department Financial Control
Business Development
Credit Control
Customer Service & Relations
Facilities & Equipment
Internal Coordination (Head
   Office/Branches)
Key Accounts
Legal Matters
Lending Policies
Market Information
Public/Community Relations
Security

Teacher/Lecturer/Professor

Administration
Budgets
Class Subjects (A, B, C, …)
Committees
Consulting Assignments
Lesson Plans
Needs Assessments
Research & Development
Student Relations & Development
Teaching Techniques
Special Projects (A, B, C, …)
Inventory/Warehouse Manager
Customer Service & Reclamations
Facilities & Equipment
Inventory Turnover
Maintenance
Packaging & Materials
Product Information
Reorder Levels
Security

Shipping Cost Control
Waste Control

Homemaker

Children
Church
Clothes
Community Affairs including
    Schools
Continuing Education
Family & Friends/Social Activities
Food/Diet
Furnishings & Equipment
Garden
Health
Hobbies
House/Apartment (Maintenance &
    Repairs)
Household Budget
Shopping
Spouse
Vacations & Recreation

Student

Career Plans
Clothing & Miscellaneous Supplies
Clubs & Student Body
Current Classes (A, B, C, ...)
Future Class Scheduling
Health & Sports Activities
Hobbies
Part-Time Work
Personal Budget
Social Events & Activities
Student Loans
Vacation Plans

Catholic Priest

Adult Bible Study
Christian Initiation of Adult
    Converts
Confraternity of Christian Doctrine
Communion Calls
Community Service
Diocesan Matters
Family & Friends
Finance Committee/Budget
Homily (Sermon) Outlines
Hospital Calls
Ideas/Innovation
Mass Stipends/Intentions
New People
Parish Council
Parish Organizations
Personal Recreation
Self-Development
Special Projects
Special Services
Staff
Youth Group

Protestant Pastor

Adult Bible Study
Community Service
Denominational Activities
Evangelism/Marketing
Executive/Board Responsibilities
Family & Friends
Finance Committee/Budget
Hospital Calls
Ideas/Innovation
Membership
Operations

Mission (Local & World)
Recreation/Fun
Self-Development
Special Projects
Special Services
Staff
Worship/Preaching
Youth Group

Military Personnel

The following list of suggested key result areas for military personnel is intended as an idea source rather than a complete listing. Depending on your duties, you may have to cover your job function and responsibilities by selecting appropriate descriptions from various headings, including the preceding listing of jobs in the private sector.

Command

Logistics
Maintenance
Supply
Morale/Welfare
Communications
Engineering
Transportation
Operations
Intelligence
Resource Management
Plans & Policies
Comptroller
Personnel

Command Security

Legal Affairs
Public Affairs
Command Security
Communication Security
Intelligence
Security Operations
Protective Services
Law Enforcement
Investigations
Corrections
Clearances

Morale/Welfare

Family Services
Religious Services
Recreation Services
Base Services
Base Exchange
Safety and Health
Mail Services

Logistics

Maintenance Management
Funds Management
Transportation Management
Readiness
Supply Operations
Freight Traffic
Shipping
Housing
Fuel Management
Emergency Supply
Installation/Site Operations
Food Services
Commercial Activities
Procurement

Facilities Services
Plant/Equipment Management
Contracting Supplies/Services

Supply
Supply Management
Property Utilization
Property Disposal
Warehousing
Requisitions/Acquisitions
Customer Service
Inventory
Document Control
Storage/Issue
Stock Control
Retail Sales
Receiving
Collections

Resource Management
Budget Analysis
Force Management
Management Analysis
Program Analysis
Studies and Reviews
Data Systems Management
Quality Control
Flight Safety
Ground Safety
Military Justice
Civil Law
Claims
Productivity
Command Inspections

Operations
Training
Instruction

Curriculum
Course Development
Scheduling
Staff Development
Simulations
Academic Services
Space Management
Disaster Preparedness
Reserve/Guard Coordination
Liaison Management

Policy and Plans
Studies/Inquiries
Mission Control
Control/Contingencies
Operations Resources
Economic Analysis
Military Manpower
Policy
Planning
Systems Integration
Automation Resources
Organization Analysis
Engineering/Technical Management
Production Quality Assessment
Tests and Standards
Evaluation and Research

Comptroller
Financial Services
Program Budget
Accounting/Finance
Internal Review
Management Information Systems
Management Engineering
Accounts Control
Funds Control

Stock Funds
Pay and Travel
Leave Accounting
Document Control

Public Affairs
Internal Information
Media Relations
Community Relations
External Information
Protocol
Information Services
Publication Services
Media Services
Telecommunications
Historian
Distribution
Programming/Scheduling

Maintenance
Maintenance Control
Job Production Control
Material Control/Support
Environmental Systems

Technical Information Management
Inspections
Repair Cycle

Personnel
Assignment/Staffing
Position Classification
Personnel Management
Evaluation
Promotions
Career Planning/Development
Transfer/Shipping
Discharge/Separation
Labor/Employee Relations
Workforce Effectiveness
Internal Development
Incentives/Awards
Job Information
Acquisition/Hiring
Training/Development
Equal Employment Opportunity
Records Management

The Geodex® Life Management System™

IN TODAY'S WORLD OF DRAMATIC CHANGE, you need a tool that motivates you to pursue your vision while being guided by your motivators and purpose. It should also be designed specifically to enable you to adjust your life and your plans to the memorable changes that come your way. You need a tool that will help you mantain an overview of your life and develop action plans to achieve your life objectives. With such a planning and change management tool, you will be in the best possible position to embrace change and fulfill your vision of success.

The Geodex Life Management System is the world's only results-driven tool specifically designed to help individuals and organizations balance work, self, and home while achieving their unique vision of success. It is much more than a time management organizer for planning meetings and maintaining schedules.

More than 100,000 Geodex users from every profession imaginable have found that using the Geodex Life Management System for a few minutes each day produces dramatic results in personal productivity, balance and happiness. It motivates them to take the time to review their progress, plan their day, and create action plans for achieving new objectives that will keep their life on track and in balance. Numerous Geodex clients have reported that this product alone is the key element to their personal and business success and that they cannot function without it.

By making the Geodex Life Management System a part of your life you can expect to:

- Gain control over your life, both in the present and, more importantly, in the future.
- Become results driven, not event or activity driven.
- Be proactive, not reactive, to life's events and their effects on you.
- Focus on effectiveness in everything you do, not merely efficiency.
- Increase your productivity by 20 percent or more, each day.
- Dramatically reduce your stress.
- Communicate better with your family and coworkers.
- Create a comfortable balance between the three spheres of influence in your life: work, self, and home.
- Feel great every day because you are on track, in control, and living a purposeful, fulfilling life.
- Achieve the success and happiness you desire.

Sample pages from the Geodex Life Management System are shown in Figures A2.1 through A2.7.

Vision, Motivators & Purpose Summary*

*(Transfer from your Lifestage Planning or Company Planning Workbook.)

Vision:

To be mature, wise, happy, and content with my chosen life path; to be at peace with my family, my community, and my work.

© Geodex International, Inc., 1997
Phone: 1-800-833-3030
ORDER # 1701

Motivators:

Balance in life   *Creativity*
Problem-solving skills   *Life fulfillment*
Integrity   *Fun*

Purpose:

To introduce to people the planning tools and techniques that promote purposeful, productive, and happy lives with a healthy balance between the needs of work, family, and self.

Reminder: For personal reference and reflection–carry this sheet in your "Life Overview" **Key Result Area**. For a company–place it in your "Workplace Overview" **Key Result Area**.

Figure A2.1   (Form shown at 80 percent of actual size)
"Vision, Motivators & Purpose Summary"

You will find it valuable to have this summary close by. By scanning it once in a while, you will motivate yourself and reinforce your chosen direction in life.

Key Result Areas Index
(Standard version)

Balance ⊛	**0**	**Life Overview**
	1	INSERT NAME OF EMPLOYER **Overview**
	2	**Financial Data & Control**
	3	**Productivity & Quality**
WORK	**4**	**Human Resources**
	5	**Customer Relations**
	6	
	7	
	8	**Self-Development**
SELF	**9**	**Health & Fitness**
	10	
	11	**Personal Finances**
	12	**Family & Lifestyle**
HOME	**13**	**Friends & Community**
	14	

© Geodex International, Inc. 1997
Phone: 1-800-833-3030
ORDER # 1017

Definition of Key Result Areas (KRA's):
"The main areas of performance and responsibility on which you must concentrate your efforts and resources in order to achieve your unique job-related and personal vision of success."

NOTE: The **Key Result Areas** on this index page have been pre-installed for your convenience and will help you to get started quickly. When you're ready to personalize your Geodex, use the included blank index page. We recommend that you re-evaluate your KRA's at least annually.

Figure A2.2

(Form shown at 80 percent of actual size)

"Key Result Areas Index (Standard version)"

We've found that these key result areas apply to 80 percent of our clients. If you're not sure about your own, start with these and then modify them later.

Key Result Areas Index

(Blank version)

WORK	**0**	*Life overview*
	1	*Geodex overview*
	2	*Financial data & control*
	3	*Team & teamwork*
	4	*Quality, productivity, service*
	5	*Marketing*
	6	*Direct sales*
	7	*Inventory & overhead control*
	8	*Plant & equipment*
	9	*Books & newsletters*
SELF	**10**	*Self-development*
	11	*Golf & fitness*
HOME	**12**	*Family & lifestyle*
	13	*House & garden*
	14	*Personal finances*

Definition of Key Result Areas (KRA's):
"The main areas of performance and responsibility on which you must concentrate your efforts and resources in order to achieve your unique job-related and personal vision of success."

NOTE: We recommend that you re-evaluate your KRA's at least annually.

Figure A2.3

(Form shown at 80 percent of actual size)

"Key Result Areas Index (Blank version)"

This is where you write in your own custom set of key result areas, as shown.

My Success Record

A written record of the Key Results that I accomplished this year towards achieving my vision of success.

Key Results Achieved: (What? How much? When?)	My Reward: (How did I reward myself or celebrate?)
Finished reengineering project on Dec. 1	*Lunch with team* *Promotion*
Landed XYZ account for $25K	*Team bonus*
Learned to speed read 1000 wpm	*Bought 2 new books*
Lowered my golf handicap to 7	*Bought new driver*
Eliminated our credit card debt	*Dinner with spouse*

NOTE: This **Success Record** is intended to be your proof and/or confirmation of success. Add to this list as you work towards your vision of success in each Key Result Area. It will make you feel good to have a permanent record of your major achievements, and can serve as a valuable resource when you need to prove your worth to yourself or others!

(Form shown at 80 percent of actual size)

Figure A2.4
"My Success Record"

Make it a point to document all your successes in life. Not only will this motivate you as you move on, it will pick you up when you're down!

Key Result Planner

KRA	11
BY	JW

PAGE	1
DATE	1/3

OBJECTIVE: (Desired Result: What / How Much / By When)

Eliminate all my credit card debt (approx. $6000) by December 31 of this year.

REWARD: (For Accomplishing Objective: What / For Whom / When)

A candlelight dinner for two on New Year's Eve.

Complete	KEY TASKS (The action steps required to meet the objective. Assign blocks of time to each one.)	Delegate To:	BUDGET[1] $ (or Cost Est.) / Time (Hr/Day/Wk)		TARGET DATES[2] Start	Review	Dead-line
☐ 1.	*Summarize last 12 months' spending*	*me*	$	Time *3 hours*	1/6		1/21
☐ 2.	*Identify all extravagant spending*	*spouse*	$	Time *1 hour*	1/21	1/22	1/23
☐ 3.	*Create a realistic budget for next 12 months*	*me*	$	Time *1 hour*	1/24	1/25	1/26
☐ 4.	*Meet with spouse & family to agree on budget*	*me*	$	Time *1/2 hour*	1/26		1/26
☐ 5.	*Find lowest interest-rate credit card available*	*me*	$	Time *1 hour*	1/26		1/28
☐ 6.	*Consolidate all debt onto new card*	*me*	$	Time *1/2 hour*	1/28		1/30
☐ 7.	*Destroy all other cards*	*spouse*	$	Time *5 min.*	1/30		1/30
☐ 8.	*Sell third car; use proceeds to pay down debt*	*me*	$ *25*	Time *5 hours*	1/25		2/10
☐ 9.	*Pay minimum $500 per month on new card*	*me*	$	Time	*monthly*		
☐ 10.	*Debt eliminated!*	*me*	$	Time			12/31

[1]TIME BLOCKS for Key Tasks transferred to Daily time planners.

[2]TARGET DATES for personal control should be transferred to Daily/Weekly/Monthly time planners.

☐ Action Plan continued on pg:

☐ For further details see BACKSIDE ➡

(vertical left margin) © Geodex International, Inc. 1997 Phone: 1-800-833-3030 ORDER # 1018 (sheets), #1062 (pads)

(Form shown at 80 percent of actual size)

Figure A2.5
"Key Result Planner" (front)

This simple form will enpower you to make detailed step-by-step action plans for each of your key result area objectives.

147

PROJECT RESOURCES	✓	Have	Need

Team Members:	Phone #:	Materials:			
		Money:			

PROBLEM PREVENTION PLANS

Area of Concern:	What Might Go Wrong?	What Should Be Done?
Time		
Team		
Materials		
Money		
Quality		
Quantity		

NOTES / DIAGRAMS / ETC.

(Form shown at 80 percent of actual size)

Figure A2.6
"Key Result Planner" (back)

The back of the Key Result Planner should be filled out for a detailed, team-based project. This will help you prevent problems from occurring.

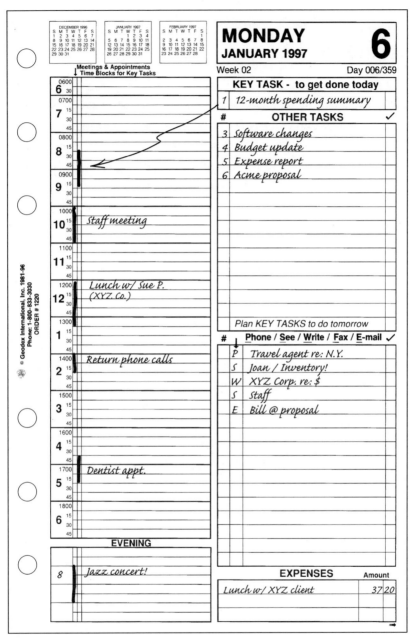

Figure A2.7
"Daily Planner"

(Form shown at 80 percent of actual size)

The daily planner is where everything comes together. Each day this will serve as your control center for what to do next.

Here's What You Get

Unlike conventional planning and organizing tools on the market, the Geodex Life Management System doesn't include ten styles of flowered calendar pages or a hundred different binder styles in five different sizes. In our experience, true high achievers care more about results. What you will receive is simply the best paper-based planning and control tool available for empowering you to realize your vision of the future. No expense has been spared in delivering a product that will help you achieve what you want in life, on your terms, with minimal clutter and complexity. If balancing all the demands in your life and coming out on top are important, then this is your solution.

Each Geodex Life Management System includes everything you need to gain balance and control in your life: handmade binder with divider tabs and plastic storage pockets, mechanical pencil, calculator, "preloaded" key result area sections, Quick Guide instructional sheets, self-starting workbook, one year's calendar materials, and a generous supply of forms and worksheets (all in 5.5- x 8.5-inch format). With this planning and change management tool, you will be in the best possible position to embrace change and fulfill your vision of success. We completely guarantee your satisfaction, for both the quality and results Geodex will deliver, for life!

Ordering Is Simple

See order form at the end of this book for complete ordering details.

1. Select a color for your binder: burgundy or black.
2. Decide whether you want an open binder or a binder with zipper closure.
3. The dated calendar material will start on the month of your choice. Please indicate your preference on the order form.

Cost: $175 for complete system with open binder, $185 for system with zipper binder.

Also Available

Customization

When ordered in quantities of 100 or more units, we are happy to customize systems, forms, and other Geodex accessories to fit your unique organizational needs. Please call for details.

Profession-Specific Versions

In addition to our universal version, we offer eleven different profession-specific modules. Please call for details.

Live Training

Please call for details.

Train-the-Trainer Program

Using the innovative Seminar-in-a-Box® program, your trainer can quickly deliver a dynamic Geodex Life Management System training session. Please call for details.

Geodex Company Planning Module

All the principles and techniques discussed in this book also apply to managing the workplace. For managers of companies, divisions, branches, and other organizations, Geodex offers a powerful strategic planning tool, the Geodex Company Planning Module: "Fast-Track Company Planning in One Day or Less." This clear and concise module empowers you to create a company plan in one day or less based upon the proven Geodex Life Management System tools, concepts, and techniques.

Why is it important to create a company plan? For every day you are not putting your best foot forward in the marketplace, your future is at risk. Given the rapid changes in our economy, greater sophistication of customers, and the ever present pressure of competition, the key challenge in business today is to recognize the spheres of influence that dominate your company (internal, external and management) and how to maintain the balance within and between them in order to achieve your vision of success and maintain growth.

Your first step is to determine the current lifestage of your company and how it affects the spheres of influence that define corporate balance, harmony, and success. This forms the basis for a dynamic strategic planning model that specifically focuses on putting your company on a balanced plan for growth and profit.

It will guide you through an evaluation process to ensure that you and your team are fully aware of the vision, core motivators, and purpose of your business. You will also consider your core competencies. Then you will focus on determining the most effective strategy or direction for you and your team to follow. The end result is a balanced company plan for achieving the company vision in all of its key result areas.

By following the recommended steps, you will have a powerful tool for managing your company for greater results. You will achieve the vision you have set for your organization with less stress, greater control, and more enjoyment. Your company will become:

- Vision- and results-driven, not event-driven
- Empowered by its core motivators
- Proactive, not reactive
- Effective, not merely efficient

Now is the time to build the foundation for successful growth and reap the rewards of the best possible combination: balanced company planning and personal life management.

Here's What You Get

The Geodex Company Planning Module includes six companion workbooks for your team, a facilitator guide, a summary workbook for the facilitator and a set of company planning forms and worksheets.

Cost: $129 for the Company Planning Module. Individual workbooks are available for $19.

About Geodex International

Geodex International is the only developer of comprehensive time, life, and company planning tools and techniques. The knowledge that we share with our clients helps them achieve balance, control, and success in all aspects of life. Geodex products are used by more than 100,000 high achievers across the country and around the world to achieve success while maintaining a balance between work, self, and home.

Contact Information

Geodex International, Inc.
P.O. Box 279
35 Maple Street
Sonoma, CA 95476

Phone
(800) 833-3030 (U.S. & Canada)
(707) 938-0001 (Local & International)

Fax
(800) 874-9549 (U.S. & Canada)
(707) 996-8734 (Local & International)

E-Mail
information@geodex.com

Web Site
www.geodex.com

Index

Varchi, Benedetto, 60
vision statement, 43–45, *143*
visualization, 108
   and crises, 117

Wall Street Journal, 91
"Work & Family" column, 91
work and success, 112
work–family conflict, 16, 20–21, 56, 99
work–family priorities, 18–19

workplace crime, 14
work roles, shifting, 8, 14
work sphere of influence, 9
world economy, 3–4
Wurman, Richard Saul, 7

yielding, 111–112
young adult transition, 37
youth lifestage, 36–37

Ziglar, Zig, 27

ORDER FORM

Four convenient ways to order:

Call: Toll free 1-800-833-3030
(U.S. & Canada, M-F, 6am-5pm PST)

Fax: Toll free 1-800-874-9549
(U.S. & Canada, Everyday, 24 hours)

Mail: Geodex International
P.O. Box 279
Sonoma, CA 95476

E-mail: Order@Geodex.com

Please send me:

_____ Life Management System, open burgundy binder @ $175 ea.

_____ Life Management System, zipper burgundy binder @ $185 ea.

_____ Life Management System, open black binder @ $175 ea.

_____ Life Management System, zipper black binder @ $185 ea.

} *Specify starting month for time planning materials.*

_____ Company Planning Module @ $129 ea.

_____ Company Planning Workbook @ $19 ea.

_____ *Life Beyond Time Management* @ $21.95 ea.

MONTH: [   ]

SUBTOTAL = _____

Shipping & Handling* = _____

7.75% Sales tax (CA only) = _____

TOTAL = _____

*Shipping & Handling
For order subtotals:
Up to $25 - $3.50
$25 to $50 - $5.50
$50 to $100 - $7.50
$100 to $200 - $9.50
$200 to $300 - $13.50
Over $300 - Add 5%
Call for overnight rates

Ship to:

Name _____

Organization _____

Street _____

City / State / Zip _____

Daytime Phone _____

Payment method:

❏ Payment enclosed (make checks payable to: Geodex International, Inc.)
❏ Charge to my Credit Card as shown below:

❏ VISA ❏ MasterCard ❏ AMERICAN EXPRESS ❏ DINERS CLUB INTERNATIONAL ❏ DISCOVER

No: [ ][ ][ ][ ] [ ][ ][ ][ ] [ ][ ][ ][ ] [ ][ ][ ][ ]

Exp. Date: _____ Signature: _____